CANADA GOOSE, WINTERING AT BLACKWATER REFUGE IN MARYLAND

CARIBOU IN SUMMER ON CALVING GROUNDS IN ARCTIC NATIONAL WILDLIFE REFUGE IN ALASKA

WILD

By Noel Grove   Photographed by Bates Littlehales
Prepared by the Special Publications Division
National Geographic Society, Washington, D. C.

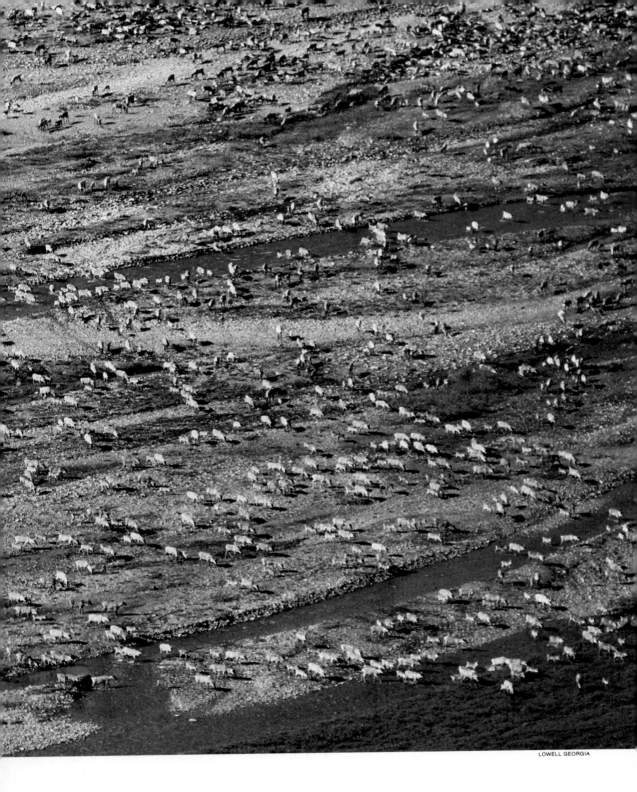

LOWELL GEORGIA

LANDS FOR WILDLIFE
AMERICA'S NATIONAL REFUGES

WILD LANDS FOR WILDLIFE:
America's National Refuges
By NOEL GROVE
Photographed by BATES LITTLEHALES

Published by THE NATIONAL GEOGRAPHIC SOCIETY
GILBERT M. GROSVENOR, *President*
MELVIN M. PAYNE, *Chairman of the Board*
OWEN R. ANDERSON, *Executive Vice President*
ROBERT L. BREEDEN, *Vice President,*
    Publications and Educational Media

Prepared by THE SPECIAL PUBLICATIONS DIVISION
DONALD J. CRUMP, *Editor*
PHILIP B. SILCOTT, *Associate Editor*
WILLIAM L. ALLEN, WILLIAM R. GRAY, *Senior Editors*

Staff for this Book
MARY ANN HARRELL, *Managing Editor*
DENNIS R. DIMICK, *Picture Editor*
JODY BOLT, *Art Director*
BARBARA A. PAYNE, *Senior Researcher and*
    Assistant to the Editor
MONIQUE F. EINHORN, *Researcher*
TONI EUGENE, SEYMOUR L. FISHBEIN,
    H. ROBERT MORRISON, CYNTHIA RUSS RAMSAY,
    GENE S. STUART, PAMELA BLACK TOWNSEND,
    Picture Legend Writers

PAMELA BLACK TOWNSEND, *Editorial Assistant*
CAROL ROCHELEAU CURTIS, *Illustrations Assistant*
PAMELA J. CASTALDI, *Assistant Designer*
JOHN D. GARST, JR., PETER J. BALCH,
    JOSEPH F. OCHLAK, *Map Research and Production*

Engraving, Printing, and Product Manufacture
ROBERT W. MESSER, *Manager*
GEORGE V. WHITE, *Production Manager*
GEORGE J. ZELLER, JR., *Production Project Manager*
MARK R. DUNLEVY, DAVID V. SHOWERS,
    GREGORY STORER, *Assistant Production Managers*
    MARY A. BENNETT, *Production Assistant*
    JULIA F. WARNER, *Production Staff Assistant*

MARY EVELYN ANDERSON, NANCY F. BERRY,
    CRICKET BRAZEROL, DIANNE CRAVEN,
    LORI E. DAVIE, MARY ELIZABETH DAVIS,
    JANET A. DUSTIN, ROSAMUND GARNER,
    VICTORIA D. GARRETT, NANCY J. HARVEY,
    JOAN HURST, ARTEMIS S. LAMPATHAKIS,
    KATHERINE R. LEITCH, CLEO E. PETROFF,
    SHERYL A. PROHOVICH, NANCY E. SIMSON,
    VIRGINIA A. WILLIAMS, *Staff Assistants*
TERESA S. PURVIS, *Indexer*

*HARDCOVER STAMP: Canada goose in flight, symbol of the
wildlife refuge system.*

Poised in courtship display, a male blue grouse at Montana's National Bison Range exposes vivid patches of neck skin called gular sacs. To attract a mate or to establish territory, the males utter a series of five or six resonant hooting sounds at frequent intervals by rhythmically inflating these sacs. The range of the blue grouse includes the western mountain states, and population density studies show no danger of extinction.

*Dwarfed by the towering snow-covered Tetons, American elk, also known
as wapiti, congregate at their lowland wintering ground in the National
Elk Refuge at Jackson, Wyoming. Truckloads of hay pellets scattered
over the 24,200-acre refuge supplement grazing for a herd of about
7,500 elk, the largest concentration of these deer in North America.*

NATIONAL GEOGRAPHIC PHOTOGRAPHER DAVID ALAN HARVEY

FOREWORD

I was raised on the Wichita Mountains National Wildlife Refuge in Oklahoma. As a small boy I woke up on summer mornings to find bison on the lawn, delighting in the several acres of green grass. Sometimes they awakened me with their peculiar snorting and snuffling sounds, and the clicking of their leg joints as they moved about. I accepted this as normal, like the presence of deer in the yard or the wild turkeys roosting in the oaks nearby. Living among wildlife was a part of my growing up; it was part of my family life.

I took for granted having wildlife as a part of my family, just as I accepted the sense of family that existed among refuge managers like my father and his fellows across the country.

Eventually I became a refuge manager myself, and though I never again lived among wild creatures in the same way I had as a boy, I learned firsthand that the family of wildlife confronts many challenges in a rapidly changing world. If our children and grandchildren are to enjoy the presence of wild animals in a wild setting—on vacations, if not from day to day—they will owe these pleasures to human forethought and care.

In 1973 I was named director of the Department of the Interior's U. S. Fish and Wildlife Service. In that job I came to realize the full meaning of our system of national wildlife refuges. I recognized more clearly the commonality of these lands—places set aside for the protection of wild animals and their habitats. I reaffirmed my conviction that refuges as distant from each other as the Hawaiian Islands and the Okefenokee are similar because they are among the last places in our country where wild creatures have priority and where the human species visits only on terms established with wildlife in mind. Some of these refuges are utterly wild, such as the Arctic National Wildlife Refuge in Alaska. Others are wild-like, but sustained only by man's intervention, like the Bosque del Apache Refuge in New Mexico, where scarce water is used with exquisite care to create an environment suitable for whooping cranes and snow geese.

Some refuges, like Red Rock Lakes in Montana, are as remote as any place can be today. Others, including the San Francisco Bay Refuge, are located within the limits of growing cities. As dissimilar as they may seem, they are a part of the family of wildlife because they provide for the varied needs of wildlife.

This book provides a glimpse of that family of wild places, and of the men and women who work there. It offers a fine insight into the refuges, the people who devote their lives to them, and into the wild creatures whose survival may depend upon them.

By LYNN A. GREENWALT,
Former Director,
U. S. Fish and Wildlife Service

Perched in the mangroves of Florida's Merritt Island Refuge, a great egret veils its nestling with the trailing nuptial plumes donned by both sexes during the breeding period. Virtually annihilated in the early 1900s, this large white heron has recovered with government protection.

A SCATTERING

OF ARKS

Away from the herd, a mature bison bull grazes placidly at Fort Niobrara National Wildlife Refuge (NWR) in Nebraska. By expert estimate, some sixty million bison once roamed North America; white explorers found them east of the Appalachians, west of the Rockies. Then guns took their toll. In 1900, federal officials reckoned just 39 wild survivors, in Yellowstone National Park. Protection has brought the United States' bison population into the thousands—with 1,200 in national refuges. A prime bull adorns the seal of the U. S. Department of the Interior, which runs the refuge system.

FOLLOWING PAGES: World-famous for beauty and for endangered status, a whooping crane rests with head upon its back. This bird has figured in a captive breeding program at Patuxent Wildlife Research Center in Maryland, which hopes to increase the free-ranging population.

LUTHER C. GOLDMAN (FOLLOWING PAGES)

The dark shapes ahead of us begin rocking like hobbyhorses as the buffalo break from a comfortable walk into a run. We are herding them across a long plateau toward a slope so steep that workers at Fort Niobrara National Wildlife Refuge call it simply "the cliff."

"We've got to push them hard when we get there," refuge manager Bob Ellis had told us back at headquarters. A lively, happy man, fond of ribbing his co-workers, he let the usual twinkle fade from his eyes as he remembered other years of moving the herd from Nebraska canyon lands to spring pastures.

"If they turn away from the cliff that first time we'll be chasing them through brush and gullies for the rest of the day."

So now, approaching the drop-off, Ellis and ten riders orchestrate a crescendo. Shrill whistles, yells, and the popping of bullwhips urge the bison on. No signals pass between the drovers, but the pace gradually picks up. The whips crack more sharply in the cold air, the yells grow louder, and from the dark sea of bobbing humps before us comes the murmur of low thunder.

My borrowed horse senses the quickening and breaks into a gallop. I glance to either side and the line of riders is holding even, wide-brimmed hats pulled tight against a slanting spring snow, yellow rain slickers flapping in the wind.

The whips pop and the yells increase—"Hyah, hy-a-a-ah." The buffalo reach full speed and my mount drops his head and points his nose forward in a dead run. Now the thunder of hooves all but drowns the cries of the men.

It flashes to me that my horse could stumble and fall, but the thought is washed away in floods of adrenalin. I yell insanely "H-A-A-A-H, HY-A-A-AH," and just before the buffalo pour over the cliff I wonder for a ludicrous instant if I have in fact died and gone to some kind of Zane Grey heaven.

My horse keeps its footing, and the buffalo negotiate the slope unharmed, as they usually do; but the thought was not far off the mark. The United States' National Wildlife Refuge System is a creator of echoes to North America's past. Throughout this nation, it has preserved—and sometimes restored—wild lands that recall a time when wild animals prevailed on the continent and man was a minority participant. These enclaves of habitat number more than 400 in 49 states, West Virginia having none; they are natural in appearance, but often are carefully managed by the U. S. Fish and Wildlife Service.

The service has nine major research stations, five specializing in fishes and four concentrating on wildlife. At Laurel, Maryland, for example, the Patuxent center documented the harmful effects of DDT in wild creatures, and thus contributed to the ban on the chemical in 1972. When species are threatened, the researchers study and initiate techniques to increase their numbers.

On the refuges, brown-shirted officers nurture plant growth that provides food and cover. Using water gates and sluices, they raise or lower pond levels to aid waterfowl production. Sometimes they oversee farming operations to create food sources replacing natural ones lost in the peopling of America.

Of all the firsts this nation is proud to claim, one of the least known and little heralded is its National Wildlife Refuge System. There's nothing like it anywhere in the world. Certainly there are large game parks in Africa, and wildlife preserves on every continent including Antarctica. But for total size, variety, and intensity of management, the U. S. refuges are unparalleled.

The smallest, Mille Lacs National Wildlife Refuge (NWR) in Minnesota, has six-tenths of an acre, the size of a suburban residential lot. The biggest, Yukon Delta NWR, is larger than West Virginia. "We jokingly call the manager there 'Governor,'" grinned affable Dave Stearns, whose own Alaskan charge, Tetlin Refuge, would nearly fill Rhode Island.

Lumped together and plopped down in the center of the U. S., the system would occupy all of Kansas plus most of Oklahoma. As they are, the refuges encompass all the major biotic zones in a nation known for geographic diversity. They vary from a low of 226 feet below sea level at Salton Sea Refuge in California to peaks exceeding 9,000 feet at Desert National Wildlife Range in Nevada. Des Lacs Refuge in North Dakota has recorded -105°F (including wind chill), while Havasu on the Arizona-California border has experienced 100 days straight at 100° or more. Annual rainfall has totaled one inch at a gauge on Kofa, in Arizona, where a cloud is nearly as rare as the sun on the Aleutian Islands, now part of the Alaska Maritime NWR.

Visiting nearly four dozen refuges, I found myself variously in swamp, desert, prairie, marsh, and forest, and on seashores, atolls, and tundra. Management of these scattered arks is a careful balance between benign neglect and deliberate manipulation.

"A lot of people think we should just fence them off and leave them natural, unaltered," said one refuge manager. "But they have already been altered by people through the farming, development, and pollution around them. There are very few natural places left in this country, especially in the lower 48."

Some people think the refuges are wasted areas. "They should have left it to the farmers," said dairyman Harvey Waas, whose acreage adjoins Horicon Refuge in Wisconsin. "Those refuge guys, they just let the land go to weeds."

One man's weed is another's game habitat. In many other ways, I found, things are seldom what they seem with the refuge system.

Take the name. They are called refuges, but more than half of them allow hunting. Managers say overcrowding and disease must be prevented in a world where man is now the main predator, but agree that "refuge" may be a misnomer. "We really should be called 'management areas,' " said one.

Many refuges have recreational facilities, but recreation is not their real business. Ultimately they exist for animals, not people.

In total acreage they are larger than the national parks, those bastions of wonder whose names spring to millions of lips—Yellowstone, Grand Canyon, Yosemite, Gettysburg. Yet few citizens know how or why refuges function.

"People hear the term 'national parks' and they think 'oh yeah, camping and hiking,' " the manager of a Texas refuge told me. "They hear 'wildlife refuge' and they think 'no-hunting signs—but what can you do there?' Many think it's some kind of zoo, with critters on display."

On a blustery March day on the Louisiana coast I started walking a nature trail that winds through the freshwater marsh of Sabine Refuge. I hadn't ambled fifty feet on the crushed-shell path when a man wearing a feed-store cap, a plaid shirt, and a worried look caught up with me. A woman and a boy lagged behind.

Was this the park built by that wild-animal place back up the road? I answered that this was the nature trail that is part of the wildlife refuge, yes.

"Huh," he said, his eyes flitting over pools fringed by cattails and cordgrass, "they told us we could see alligators and everything out here."

It was midmorning, when many creatures have either gone into hiding till dusk or flown to distant feeding grounds. Patience, however, and a sharp eye will reveal those that remain. Plaid Shirt trudged unseeing near a full-grown nutria that quietly climbed ashore among the reeds and began grooming itself. A group of northern shoveler ducks sweeping their broad bills through the water, straining plankton, rated a glance, as did a dabbling family of coots. Hurrying past a statue-still egret he failed

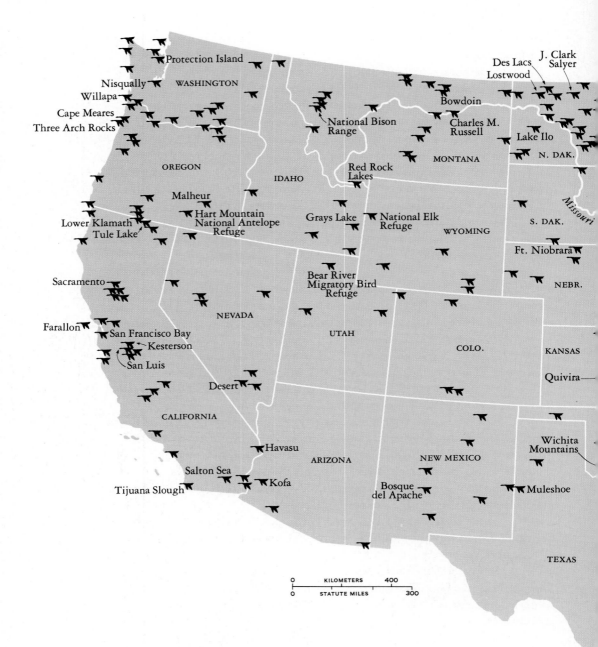

"Blue goose" logo—actually, a Canada goose in flight, official symbol since 1935—marks national wildlife refuges across the continent. (A map of Alaska appears on page 185.) Insets show Caribbean refuges, and Hawaii. Far in the central Pacific, not shown here, lie five others: on Johnston, Jarvis, Howland, and Baker Islands, and Rose Atoll in American Samoa. Spread from the tropics to the Arctic, including about 90 million acres, and intensively managed, the National Wildlife Refuge System of the United States has no parallel on earth.

Hawaiian

Agassiz
MINN.
Tamarac
Mille Lacs
WISCONSIN
Minnesota
Valley
Upper Mississippi
Seney
Necedah
Horicon
MICH.

IOWA
DeSoto

ILL.
IND.
OHIO
MISSOURI

OKLA.
Mingo
Reelfoot
TENN.
Wheeler
ARKANSAS
ALA.
MISS.
LA.

Attwater
Prairie
Chicken
Sabine
Lacassine
Breton   St. Vincent

Aransas

Santa Ana

KY.

Montezuma

Great Swamp
PA.
DEL.
MD.
Patuxent
W. VA.
VA.
Presquile

ME.
Moosehorn

Seal Island

VT.
N.H.
Parker River
N.Y.
Monomoy
MASS.
R.I.
CONN.
Trustom Pond

N.J.
Brigantine

Blackwater
Chincoteague

Pea Island
Mattamuskeet
N.C.

Carolina Sandhills
S.C.

Piedmont
GA.
Wassaw
Blackbeard Island
Okefenokee

Lake Woodruff
Merritt Island
FLA.
Pelican Island

J. N. "Ding" Darling

National Key Deer
Refuge

PUERTO RICO AND
U. S. VIRGIN ISLANDS

HAWAIIAN ISLANDS
Hanalei
Islands N.W.R.

17

to see its lightning thrust at a fish, and he walked within fifteen feet of a seven-foot gator lying still as a log.

When I caught up with him later, waiting morosely while the woman and boy read a placard about marsh habitat, I asked him if he'd seen anything. He lifted his shoulders in a disappointed shrug: "Bunch'a ducks."

It was a diminishing bunch of ducks that transformed America's wildlife refuges from a miscellany of "game preserves" to a chain of wild lands. President Theodore Roosevelt had created the first one in 1903 when he set aside little three-acre Pelican Island in Florida to protect nesting birds from trigger-happy humans. Two more followed, also for birds. Oklahoma's Wichita Mountains were designated in 1905 as a home for rapidly disappearing buffalo, as was the National Bison Range in Montana in 1908. Sanctuaries for elk and pronghorn antelope followed, and thus the principle of using federal lands to protect endangered wildlife was established.

Needed was the impetus for a large-scale system. It blew in on an ill wind—the dust storms of the "dirty thirties."

Drought, and the drainage of wetlands for agriculture, had dried up thousands of the northern ponds, sloughs, and marshes where waterfowl produce their young each spring. An army of duck hunters with liberal bag limits threatened to pick off the remainder. But the clamor of some hunters and a few dedicated conservationists resulted in the "Duck Stamp Law" of 1934.

By purchasing a stamp to be affixed to their hunting permits, sportsmen provided funding that helped set aside wetlands for waterfowl. Some 635,000 of the first year's stamps were sold at $1 each, and sales had topped a million a year by 1940, at a time when wetlands could be bought for as little as $1 an acre.

Before duck stamps, a total of 120 refuges had been established. From March 1934 through 1941, another 180 were added. Not surprisingly, many of them lay along the four major routes of the North American flyways and 77 of them were in North Dakota, potholed with small ponds used by nesting ducks and geese.

"The refuge system used to be known as a duck outfit," a refuge manager told me, "and the name was deserved. Duck predators like skunks and foxes were shot and trapped. Now we try to establish a more balanced wild community."

In fact, these biological islands harbor virtually every wild mammal, bird, reptile, and fish native to this continent. Several endangered species owe their continued existence to the refuge lands.

Awkwardly enough, the refuge system is not a separate bureau as are the National Park and the National Forest Services. No single law spells out its duties and methods. The refuge system is a division (Refuge Management) within a bureau (Fish and Wildlife) within a department (Interior)—the bureaucratic equivalent of having an in-box but not a whole desk. Often funding and direction are influenced by other units such as Endangered Species, Research and Development, or Migratory Birds.

The strongest critics of the refuge system—who are also its greatest admirers—fear that this fragmentation weakens its ability to operate.

"Fish and Wildlife has so many diverse responsibilities that it cannot direct its full attention to the refuge system," said Forrest Carpenter, head of the National Wildlife Refuge Association. This is a private group that sees itself as a watchdog to defend the refuges from their own government. "The absence of a dominant position in the FWS structure and the lack of an organic law describing refuge responsibilities have a fracturing effect on the whole system."

Fractured though it may be, it is a fractured diamond, "the gemstone of Fish and Wildlife," as a policymaker in Washington headquarters put it. Keepers of the gleam are the nearly 1,900 Fish and Wildlife employees—just over a fourth of all bureau personnel—who are directly associated with refuges.

Most refuges have a manager, an assistant manager, a secretary or two, and—if visitation is heavy—a public use officer. Many have a full-time biologist. At least one maintenance-and-improvising worker keeps vehicles and equipment operating. On a large, complex refuge there may be several biological technicians, often college graduates who want to work their way up to the driver's seat.

"Running a refuge is the pinnacle of wildlife management," said one manager proudly. "But that creates a problem. A lot of good managers don't want to be promoted to regional level or to Washington and lose their work on a refuge."

The thrill of success, as usual, is diminished by realities of drudgery.

"We all envision entering this line of work to commune with the peeping deer and the tinkling waterfall," said manager Tom Atkeson, sometime poet and veteran of 45 years at Wheeler Refuge in Alabama. "Instead we find ourselves buried under an avalanche of paperwork."

More paperwork will be necessary as civilization's needs conflict with nature's. Refuges often include riches in petroleum, timber, minerals, water, and grazing coveted by private stockmen. Oil was being pumped or drained from 23 refuges in 1983, and timber sales totaled $1,186,143.06.

As Secretary of the Interior in the early 1980s, James Watt urged additional economic development on refuge lands—and raised a storm of protest from environmentalists. In July 1983 the National Audubon Society devoted 82 pages of its bimonthly magazine to the refuges, warning that current policy and private pressures were seriously undermining efforts to preserve wildlife habitat. Yet an officer in the society agreed that the pressures would have occurred had there never been a James Watt (who resigned in October 1983).

"It would be better to focus on the vulnerability of the refuge system than on one individual," said the officer, Dave Cline of Alaska. "Pressures to develop refuge resources will only intensify, and better laws are needed to define how the refuges can be better defended."

Robert Gilmore, deputy associate director of the system when I met him in 1983, denies that refuges have been hindered in any way. "I challenge any refuge manager armed with good solid facts to show me where he or she has ever been rolled over on a decision favoring people over wildlife," he told me with some heat. "The difference is in the data they have. That's why we are pushing our people to get good hard data on what wildlife needs and how development, hunting, or visitation would affect them. If you don't have good data, development will win, almost every time."

"I remind my younger colleagues sometimes that the U. S. has been occupied by non-natives only 500 years, and intensively occupied only 200, and wildlife habitat seriously affected in only the last two generations," said Lynn Greenwalt, former head of the Fish and Wildlife Service and now a vice president of the National Wildlife Federation. "This is a sprawling country, and not until very recently did people realize that a real confrontation was taking place with wildlife."

By then, whole communities of wildlife established over thousands of years had been erased. The ax and the plow have been more destructive than the gun, but attitude has been the grimmest reaper of all.

"In the 18th century man seemed determined to prove that he was different from the animals," said Stephen Kellert, professor of social ecology at Yale. "Killing wildlife and replacing its habitat with productive croplands was a part of that feeling."

How efficiently it was done. The American bison plummeted from millions to hundreds, as every schoolchild knows, and the passenger pigeon whose flocks once darkened the skies lightened them with its total disappearance. Wolves, once found from coast to coast, number fewer than 1,500 in the lower 48 states.

Despite our misuses Americans have a special fondness for wildlife, according to an extensive study by Kellert. "We found that Americans consider wildlife a part of their heritage, although they don't know much about the animals themselves or what they need. Their fondness for wildlife is selective, however. They like large creatures—expressive, intelligent animals. And they believe that wildlife should earn its way by providing benefits to people."

Sometimes that belief in benefits extends beyond the law. Poaching is a problem on many refuge lands. I spent hours with workers patrolling at night. Overtime work? "We just call that donated time," drawled a western officer.

Illegal hunting is only one of the reasons why refuge workers often carry a gun. I had one placed in my hand one day as a frightening scene unfolded.

A hysterical young escapee from a mental institution was threatening to injure himself if a federal officer came any closer. Suddenly the patient drew a pistol and fired point-blank at the officer, who collapsed. Too late, I fired in return. A small hole appeared at the young man's shoulder and he froze . . .

Rather, his image froze, on a movie screen at the Federal Law Enforcement Training Center (FLETC) near Brunswick, Georgia. Some fifty refuge officers annually attend a nine-week course here, learning to deal with situations realistic enough to elicit a cold sweat. I was taking part in "judgment pistol shooting," filmed dramatizations of actual incidents, designed to sharpen officers' reactions in emergencies. Sequence after sequence demands a split-second life-or-death decision. A projectile fired through the replaceable paper screen freezes the projector, allowing both the trainee and the instructor to assess the results.

"We're not only testing their judgment, we're trying to develop it," said instructor Kent Williams, who helped design the pistol shoot. "Is that a criminal reaching for a gun, or an innocent citizen reaching for identification? You have to be quick. He *knows* what he is going to do."

Spacious, unoccupied, sometimes remote, refuges become sites for beer busts, drug deals, homicides, illegal entry by aliens. For the most part, however, they are islands of calm in an increasingly crowded world. There are refuges adjoining great cities, others at the edge of housing tracts or shadowed by the smokestacks of manufacturing, and many surrounded by farmland.

This book groups the refuges according to ecological regions. One fits in nearly all of them. A jeweled oasis, a swatch of primal green in the midst of gray soil and row cropping, little Santa Ana Refuge west of Brownsville, Texas, holds the kind of problems, promise, and pleasures found in most refuges.

"We're an eco-crossroads," said Melvin Maxwell, outdoor recreation planning officer, a man mesquite-tough to match the 2,088 acres of chaparral brush he helps oversee along the Rio Grande. "We have climatic influences from the coast east of us and the Chihuahuan Desert to the west. It's tropical to the south, prairie to the north, and yet our vegetation makes us look like a woodland."

A border refuge, Santa Ana encounters border troubles. One young man was arrested trying to pick up drugs delivered from Mexico; in another incident, the Border Patrol arrested four illegal aliens. But such episodes go virtually unnoticed by most of the 100,000 visitors a year.

Main attractions are tropical birds from Mexico, whose range reaches the border. Staff biologist Steve Labuda led me to a photographic blind where we peeked at emerald-colored green jays, golden-fronted woodpeckers, and the Altamira oriole, brilliant orange with a black cape. Walking the paths early the next day, we spotted a great kiskadee perched on a branch near a small stream, a rascally-looking fellow wearing a dark mask. We were bombarded by cacophonies of chachalacas, mistakenly called Mexican pheasants. Their name resembles their raucous call, a shriek that seems to celebrate the survival of another night of prowling coyotes, bobcats, and ocelots.

With intensive use of such a small area, accommodations must be made for both people and animals. A concrete nature trail for the handicapped levels out every sixty feet so wheelchair operators can rest. A low curbing on one side guides the blind, who can smell the rich dankness of rotting vegetation, touch the long needle-like leaves of the retama tree, hear the chatter and dabble of shorebirds in the mud of a small lagoon.

"Since 1978 public visitation here has increased about 10 percent a year," said the amiable Melvin Maxwell. He was referring to a change that affects other accessible refuges, and implies new problems. To cut down on car traffic, Santa Ana hauls many visitors in a quiet cutaway bus called a tram. I joined a tram-load of "snowbirds"—retired northerners who migrate in winter to the endless summer along the Rio Grande—to hear tour guide Kathy Duncan's low-toned commentary.

"There are chachalacas in the brush to your right."

"There they are, Rosie, do you see 'em?"

"Those little shells are tree snails, eaten by the roadrunner. He can't break them on the ground so he puts them on a rock and pecks them open."

"Well I'll be doggoned."

The tram pulled onto a levee that marked the refuge's northern boundary: long symmetrical crop rows on one side and on the other a tangle of huisache bushes, prickly pear cactus, mesquite, and tall tepeguaje trees.

Kathy spoke again: "As you can see, on this side we have an area that looks perfectly natural, while over here is land under heavy agricultural use."

A retired farmer, face ruddy from decades of fieldwork, looked from one to the other. Foliage or factories? Wild creatures or crops?

Wildlife survives outside America's national refuges—in national parks and forests, in state game preserves, and on private holdings. The National Audubon Society maintains sanctuaries of its own, and the Nature Conservancy buys strategic parcels of habitat, sometimes entrusting them to the refuge system for safekeeping.

Yet the national system is crucial: its research capabilities, its highly trained personnel, its federal funding. The national refuges are modern man's greatest acknowledgment that wild creatures have a rightful place on this planet. Rather than losing space, we gain a perspective, according to Kellert.

"This is a high-pressure world, all speed and stress," says the Yale ecologist, "and we are split in so many ways. With wildlife, people get a sense of peace and solitude, a natural way of dealing with life. Besides, it's intrinsically beautiful!"

The beauty does not leap at you as from a good painting or photograph. It is not confined and waiting for you, as in a zoo. Enjoyment often requires patience, silence, and the realization that dawn and dusk are prime viewing times.

You will not be pampered when you come here, for the refuge is their world. You are a visitor, a student, and a beneficiary. A doe's leaping flight through a foggy glade is a study in grace. The wingbeats of the snow goose can sweep cobwebs from the most cluttered mind.

Alert but unafraid, female mule deer—perhaps a mother and yearling—drift through early morning fog to the shelter of Douglas fir on Red Rock Lakes Refuge in Montana. Rocky Mountain iris blossom in early summer by Tom Creek in the marshes of the valley floor. This habitat offers the isolation required by trumpeter swans, rare when the government founded this refuge for them in 1935, now fairly abundant. Traces of winter's deep snowpack linger in July on the Centennial Mountains.

Down the hatchling goes, just hours old, lured to water by its mother's calls. The wood duck babies at New Jersey's Great Swamp NWR may drop 10 or 20 feet, splash, and swim off, a dozen or so to the brood. The hens took easily to boxes when natural nest sites—hollow trees—grew scarce. The box design includes a cone to thwart raccoons and other raiders. Citizens fought off a jetport planned for this area and preserved Great Swamp as habitat for more than 200 species of birds.

Absolutely still, a mallard hen and her brood "freeze" on their downy nest to escape detection at the National Bison Range in Montana. Best known and perhaps most abundant of ducks in North America, mallards can hold the freeze posture at length. If an intruder comes too close they flush—the young scatter, diving into water or hiding among reeds, while the mother distracts the predator by a so-called "broken-wing" display. With one refuge created just for buffalo, the system has acquired some 7,700,000 acres for migratory birds; and funds earned by selling duck stamps to hunters—more than $270,000,000 since 1934—have covered much of the cost.

Lesser snow geese and greater sandhill cranes mingle in November at Bosque del Apache NWR in New Mexico. The sandhills migrate south from Grays Lake NWR in Idaho; some 30 whooping cranes fly with them. Both whoopers and snow geese have white plumage with black wingtips, so the hunting season demands strict control. Goose hunters must pass a recognition test to shoot on the refuge, but need only a license and duck stamp nearby. Also, birds swallowing grit to aid digestion may take in lead shot as well as gravel. A young whooper died of lead poisoning here in early 1984. Environmentalists call for an end to hunting at Bosque, and for the use of nontoxic steel shot everywhere.

Drip torch in hand, a refuge staff man sets a planned fire at Blackwater, on Maryland's Eastern Shore. Controlled burning leaves the wet soil unaffected but consumes dead marsh vegetation, stimulating early growth of three-square. These bulrushes, named for a three-sided stem, help feed 35,000 wintering ducks and 65,000 Canada geese. Blackwater Refuge gives year-round sanctuary to bald eagles; golden eagles come for the winter.

Little bird, big egg—clearly a mismatch. Will nature permit nurture? Likely not, say officials at J. Clark Salyer Refuge, where the black tern faces an egg nearly twice the size of its own. Perhaps a gull or grebe laid the egg and abandoned it; both species nest amid the river bulrushes and cattails (opposite, below). Here farmers dreaming of rich harvests dried wetlands and broke the prairie sod. The land resisted; crops failed. The refuge, established in 1935, diked the Souris River and reflooded the valley. Today watergates like the one opposite help maintain the marshes, making Salyer a major stop on the Central flyway—and a big contributor to North Dakota's ranking as the top producer of ducks in the 48 contiguous states.

A spacious tract of native habitat on the lower Rio Grande in south Texas, Santa Ana NWR draws birders and botanists to its unique tropical ecosystem. Shaded by cedar elms and Spanish moss, former manager Ray Rauch shows students its living treasures—like the green jay (above), long since vanished from the surrounding farmland.

PRECEDING PAGES: A prime desert bighorn ram runs up brush-filled Twin Spires Canyon on the Kofa in southwestern Arizona—a 660,000-acre refuge established in 1939 for the protection and increase of this species.

"Under siege"—so officials sum up the state of things at Tijuana Slough NWR in California. Above, a visitor breaks regulations to hunt ghost shrimp for fishing bait; terns and gulls take wing while a marbled godwit (left) searches for food in nearby shallows. Beyond the marsh, Imperial Beach Boulevard marks the southern edge of the San Diego metropolis, whose residents want more recreation areas. Just to the south lies the Mexican border; "illegals" headed north cross the refuge frequently. Navy pilots in noisy helicopters practice homing over the area— "impact on wildlife undetermined." Refuge staff must try "to regulate uses and balance demands."

White wings flared, a pair of great egrets threaten a great blue heron that has come too close to an unfinished nest; an olivaceous cormorant adds its threat display. All three species nest in two bald cypress groves at Lacassine NWR in southwestern Louisiana. On nearby Sabine Refuge, a drilling crew conveyed by marsh buggies runs a seismic survey, firing explosives underground to search for oil. If carefully done, this causes little permanent damage. Following a channel cut through the refuge, an 810-foot oil tanker churns toward the Gulf. The channel lets salt water invade the freshwater marsh, gradually destroying large areas of essential habitat. In July 1984 a British tanker ran aground offshore and began leaking her cargo: millions of gallons of crude—a threat to Sabine and other refuges.

DAVID CUPP (ABOVE AND TOP); N.G.S. PHOTOGRAPHER BATES LITTLEHALES (LEFT)

41

Scanning the shallows for a crab or a crawfish, a yellow-crowned night heron hunts among the mangroves of J. N. "Ding" Darling Refuge in southwestern Florida. This refuge honors the noted conservationist who administered wildlife programs under the New Deal. Brown pelicans flourish today at little Pelican Island, all of three and a half acres at low tide. President Theodore Roosevelt set it aside for them as a sanctuary in 1903—first of the national wildlife refuges, with a warden whose salary came to one dollar a month. Today it comes under the supervision of staff at the Merritt Island Refuge.

FARRELL GREHAN (ABOVE); N.G.S. PHOTOGRAPHER BATES LITTLEHALES (OPPOSITE)

Family farming protects four endangered species of Hawaiian birds on the 917 acres of floodplain and wooded hillsides that make up Hanalei Refuge on Kauai. Taro growers maintain impoundments of shallow water for their cuttings at just the depth—four to six inches—preferred by the ae'o, *or Hawaiian stilt. At left, stilts forage for food in a habitat becoming rare outside the Hanalei Valley. Other species enjoying this refuge: the* koloa maoli, *"native duck," the* 'alae ke'oke'o, *or Hawaiian coot, and the* 'alae 'ula, *or Hawaiian gallinule. Below, varying shades of green reveal taro at different stages of growth. The Hanalei River flows from Mount Waialeale, rainiest spot on earth with an average 486 inches a year.*

Seabirds and sea mammals crowd cliffs and shores of Togiak Refuge in Alaska. Some 7,000 walruses have hauled out to rest at Cape Peirce (right). Bulls, bigger than cows and coated with bumps (below), will wield their tusks to bully their way to choice beach spots. Bristles detect shellfish underwater when walruses feed offshore, where nesting birds of Cape Newenham (below, left) also find sustenance. Bounteous Beringian waters—the Bering Sea here and the Chukchi Sea to the north—support an imposing density of marine bird and mammal life. And across its vastness the largest state contains nearly nine of every ten acres in the National Wildlife Refuge System: unspoiled terrain for lordly grizzlies, room to roam for caribou, breeding grounds for tens of millions of birds.

ALL BY STEVEN C. KAUFMAN

COASTS

AND ISLANDS

Winter's cyclic fury strews shells and spindrift at Pea Island, a refuge on North Carolina's Outer Banks. Since 1938 this barrier-isle reserve has welcomed greater snow geese wintering at the southern limit of their range, and other migrants as well. Local shorebirds nest here in spring and summer. Such undeveloped coasts and wild shores remain desirable for commerce and recreation— but essential for wildlife survival.

FOLLOWING PAGES: An osprey in Florida's Merritt Island NWR clutches a fish. In the 1960s, DDT in the food chain threatened these and other birds; ospreys have recovered well, with careful management and a federal ban on the powerful pesticide.

When darkness came we hit the beach, the jeep growling over the dunes and onto the hard-packed sand. Ahead lay a long night of patrolling the shores of Wassaw Island off the Georgia coast, looking for telltale tracks headed inland. I had joined a group of environmental guerrillas whose mission was to defend the invading forces, not repel them.

Each summer female loggerhead turtles, armored creatures weighing from 150 to 300 pounds, lumber ashore to lay some 120 eggs apiece in the warm sand.

"Ghost crabs tunnel down to the eggs and eat a few, and then raccoons dig up the nests," said the jeep driver, Win Seyle. The 29-year-old biologist helps run a turtle rescue program sponsored by the Savannah Science Museum and the Fish and Wildlife Service. "Even those that hatch and dash down the beach may be picked off by predators. And if they make it to the sea they can be eaten by anything with a mouth this big," Win added, his thumb and forefinger about two and a half inches apart.

An old and often quoted estimate says that one in every thousand sea turtle hatchlings survives to adulthood. Today specialists suspect that's too optimistic a figure. The one authority willing to suggest a substitute says, "Maybe one in some thousands." Poor odds in any case, worsened now by human pressures. Housing projects and recreation areas frighten mother turtles away from their traditional nesting grounds, and may lure the babies away from ocean waters.

"White glow from the surf may be what attracts turtles back to sea," said Win. "We know the lights of houses and marinas can draw them off course."

Other species have been thrown off course by the human love of seaside property. Important biological changes take place where land and sea meet. Tidal currents bring in organisms essential to shorebirds, then wash out food for fish waiting offshore. Salt marshes are nurseries for young marine life, winter feeding grounds for hosts of ducks and geese.

Coastal plenty impressed the early European settlers. Near Jamestown, Virginia, in 1607, colonist George Percy observed an "abundance of Fowles of all kindes, they flew over our heads as thicke as drops of Hale; besides they made such a noise, that wee were not able to heare one another speake."

Ever since, the richness of coastal life has fascinated Americans. Surrounding inlets with cities, lining beaches with vacation houses, dredging marshes to make marinas, we've loved our shores nearly to death.

Like a necklace worn to recall days of virgin beauty, a string of refuges beads the nation's coasts and islands. More than fifty are touched by Atlantic waters alone, and often their names evoke Indian history and maritime romance: Monomoy, Chincoteague, Brigantine, Blackbeard Island.

Many serve principally as way stations for migrating waterfowl; others have purposes and functions as varied and colorful as their names. Seal Island off Maine harbors pelagic—seagoing—birds and has always been closed to the public; a former bombing-and-bombardment range for the Navy, it also harbors live explosives. Thousands of people, on the other hand, annually visit Chincoteague to see the wild ponies made famous by the children's book about a filly named Misty. And Wassaw Island protects open beach for nesting sea turtles.

Birds, deer, small mammals, and a fair number of alligators make Wassaw their permanent home. I saw my first painted bunting, perhaps our most brilliantly colored songbird, as I walked a leaf-strewn path lined with live oaks and slash pine. Development never touched here because a family named Parsons owned the 5-by-³/₄-mile island as a vacation retreat for more than a century; they kept the family compound when the refuge system acquired the rest.

Now participants in the turtle program pay $250 for an arduous privilege: a week of all-night patrols to protect freshly laid eggs and, later, fresh hatchlings. They include teachers, biology hobbyists, and prep school students attracted to a week of island adventure with a dash of good deeding thrown in. Tough duty—tougher still when the turtles don't cooperate.

"We've had a late, cool spring," offered refuge manager John Hoffmann after several nights of no-shows. "That must be keeping them away."

Six more turtleless hours passed one evening when high tide forced our vehicles off the beach. Susan Arnold of Hawkinsville, Georgia, a veteran patroller, scorned resting back at the Parsons' cabins. "I came to find turtles, not take naps," she said in a broad Georgia accent, and talked her 16-year-old nephew Lee into joining her in a foot patrol. Shamed into action, I went along.

It was Susan who found a nesting turtle. "Quiet now," she whispered. "She can be spooked while she's still diggin' the nest. When she starts layin' the eggs you could hold a square dance on her shell and she wouldn't leave."

With one hind flipper, then the other, a yard-long loggerhead scooped out a light-bulb-shaped hole in the sand. Then she dipped the back of her carapace into the cavity and began straining. Behind her, where I had brushed away sand to observe, eggs shaped like table-tennis balls dropped into the hole.

I turned the flashlight on her head to see tears streaming from her eyes. They throw off excess salt acquired at sea, but it is hard to escape the illusion that she is crying—for what? The fate of so many hundred offspring?

After a quarter hour of egg-laying she swept sand into the hole with her flippers, then labored back toward the sea. Intercepting her, we tipped her onto her broad back for measurement and tagging. "Information on sea turtles is so sketchy," Win had said. "We see them when they hatch; we see them as adults nesting or when they're washed up dead on the beach. In between we don't know much about where they go or what they do."

We righted the 250-pounder and watched her scurry back to water. Her leathery eggs were dug up and reburied at a spot beyond the reach of extremely high tides; a screen cover would keep out crabs and raccoons. Sixty days later, other volunteers would escort the hatchlings as they fast-flippered down the beach.

Time seems to pause on unspoiled Wassaw. It leaps the centuries on another island I visited. In tidewater Virginia, inland 72 river miles from the mouth of the James, lies a refuge called Presquile. In French *presqu'île* means peninsula, but in 1934 a navigational channel made an island of it—in fact, and in ecology as well.

The approach to the refuge is on Allied Chemical Road, past industrial plants billowing smoke from high stacks. Refuge manager Harold Olson brought a ferry across the channel to pick me up.

"It's not much different from what was here before," he said as we chugged across. "Of the 1,329 acres on the island, 800 are swamp and 250 are marsh. A local farmer grows 140 acres of wheat here, which gives the geese green browse in winter. The rest is woodland."

Ten thousand ducks, as many Canada geese, and a few hundred snows and blues make Presquile their winter home. Some stray to private lands across the James, but soon learn that the guns bark nearly everywhere except the refuge. Deer are the only game hunted here, to maintain herd size. There are foxes, squirrels, rabbits, and the ring-tailed tree-dweller the Powhatan Indians called *aroughcun,* now known as raccoon. Walking a path used by school groups on field trips, I startled a pair of wood ducks, gaudy beauties that like quiet woodland pools. Vultures, hawks, and ospreys soar above the island, and eagles are making a comeback. "The area had its first nesting pair in years in 1981," said Harold.

The effect of DDT on wildlife, particularly eagles, was widespread. The James suffered a unique calamity when fifty tons of the pesticide Kepone were dumped in the river between 1966 and the mid-seventies. "Right around that bend, almost within sight of the refuge," said Harold, pointing south. "Much of it has been covered up with silt, but sportsmen are still advised that they eat fish from here at their own risk."

We were looking across the wheat field toward the billowing smokestacks. Something massive crept out of the tree line to our right, a metal mountain. An ocean-going cargo ship was steaming through the channel, bound from Richmond to Izmir, Turkey. Gliding noiselessly across the landscape, it blotted out the factories and towered over a plaque that marks the location of Bermuda Hundred, a half-forgotten shipping point settled as early as 1613. Yesterday and today, staring each other in the face.

Factories and pollution are dramatic examples of the present. At Blackwater Refuge in Maryland, change is measured in shifting grains of silt.

Subsidence of the coastline is the natural factor here; a road that cuts across the refuge and alters the flow of runoff is the man-made complication. Where silt washes away, marsh vegetation vanishes. By December 65,000 geese and 35,000 ducks may be winging over this refuge near Chesapeake Bay, but their habitat is in trouble. While other areas struggle against siltation, Blackwater is trying to increase it.

One chilly morning the refuge motorboat took me up broad Blackwater River to see the rebuilding of a marsh. High school students working in the federally funded Youth Conservation Corps had ringed a barely submerged mud flat with straw bales. Mud was then pumped in to raise the ground level. Wading into the muck, the teenagers hand-planted roots and rhizomes of bulrush to anchor the silt.

"Since 1938 we've lost 3,000 acres," said biological technician Guy Willey, who has seen much of it happen in his three decades at the refuge. "We hope barriers like this will slow down the water so the marsh will rebuild itself."

"Crocodilians have tremendously strong muscles for closing their jaws but very weak ones to open them. A strong man can hold a crocodile's jaws shut barehanded." So read the "fun facts" in the comic books and bubble-gum wrappers of my youth. I was fascinated but skeptical. Is that why I found myself astraddle a seven-foot alligator one night in a Louisiana marsh, my fingers in a death grip around the bones of its lower jaw?

For my companions it was all in a night's work. For 18 months the officers at Lacassine Refuge in coastal Louisiana had been lassoing alligators, wrestling them onto an airboat, and—yes—holding their mouths shut while they placed tags in the webbing between the reptiles' toes.

"In the mid-sixties our gators were just about wiped out by overhunting," said refuge manager Bobby Brown. "They're coming back, but to protect them we've got to understand them."

How fast does an alligator grow? How far does it range?

And protecting the local wildlife requires a certain understanding of the hunters as well as the hunted. License plates declare the state a "sportsman's paradise," for the marshes and bayous have long been rich with waterfowl, muskrats, fish, and deer as well as alligators. Many bayou dwellers whose forebears lived off the land find it hard to accept any restrictions on their hunting.

Yet the image of hard-bitten game warden would be off the mark for most refuge officers, as it is for this soft-spoken manager who paints and woodsculpts wildlife in his off-hours.

"I heard shots one night and boated to a camp—a houseboat—and saw men butchering deer out of season," he told me. "They started throwing the carcasses into the river so I gunned my motor and tried to run up on the porch but my boat bounced off. When I jumped from my boat onto theirs I slipped and would have fallen into the river if one of them hadn't grabbed me." He grinned sheepishly. "I knew then that I wasn't exactly dealing with desperate men."

The five were fined $750 each plus court costs and forbidden to hunt in Louisiana for a year.

Nighttime goose hunts are also a thorn in Bobby Brown's side. Lacassine's 16,000 acres of natural marsh and 16,000 of diked impoundment winter nearly three-quarters of a million waterfowl. I joined him in January for several nights of motorboat patrols; we zipped around with lights out to catch the sweep of spotlights, or silenced the engine to listen for shots. We heard nothing but the doll-like cries of nutria, caught nothing but chills. "If you want to see some action," he said, "come back when we're tagging alligators." And that's how I ended up on the back of America's dragon.

The first we lassoed was a nine-footer whose eyes flashed amber when assistant manager Charlie Hebert swept a powerful spotlight across the water. The gator crash-dived at our approach but was visible on the bottom, four feet below. Charlie slipped a pole under its head and pried it off the mud until a partner could slip a metal noose behind the massive jaws. Then Charlie took over the stout staff that held the noose and gave a heave on the thick wire cable.

The water boiled as the reptile surged to the surface, mouth agape to fight whatever had a grip on its neck. Writhing, whipping, it attacked the boat and the long white teeth clanged on metal. It twisted like a corkscrew, splashing water over all of us. "They have tremendous bursts of energy but only for a short time," said Charlie.

Finally the gator let itself be hauled onto the broad hull of the airboat. Charlie slammed its mouth shut with the heel of his hand, gripped both sides to hold it shut, and swung onto its back. "Jump on behind me," he cried, "and put all your weight on it or it'll back us right into the water."

The legs churned, the claws dug futilely for purchase, and the snout hissed outrage. We tagged it, measured it, and determined its sex—male—before letting it splash back into the water, one of nine we caught that night.

Before an international treaty and federal law restricted the sale of hides, Louisiana's alligators were in trouble. That they didn't disappear is partly due to John Walther, manager for 21 years at Sabine Refuge.

"In the '60s we kept four people in the marsh every night between March and October," said Walther, a round-faced man with laughing eyes. "During the day we walked around in a daze, but we kept the gators. Eventually ours helped stock the rest of Louisiana, so now there're hunting seasons on them again."

Down where the East Coast ends is a refuge set up to stop the hunting of an animal that looks like a child's toy, the diminutive deer peculiar to the Florida Keys. A full-grown buck might measure a little over two feet tall at the shoulders. A fawn could stare eye to eye at a large jackrabbit.

Nearly extinct at midcentury from hunting and loss of habitat, these little whitetails were saved by the establishment of National Key Deer Refuge in 1954. At sunrise and sunset, hoping for a glimpse, I prowled palmetto thickets and visited the water holes in limestone depressions.

Finally a doe and fawn dashed across the road. They paused a few seconds for a backward look, then quickly pranced on.

A similar scene, vividly drawn, had done much to save the Key deer. The artist was J. N. Darling of Iowa's *Des Moines Register,* who signed his cartoons "Ding." His cartoon of glowering bullies running down a tiny trio—doe, fawn, and stag—goaded the nation to outrage. A conservationist ahead of his time, Darling served for nearly two years in the early 1930s as a chief of the Bureau of Biological Survey, a predecessor of today's Fish and Wildlife Service, and refused to accept a salary.

Now Sanibel Island, off Florida's west coast, holds the J. N. "Ding" Darling Refuge, a fitting tribute to this pioneer in wildlife awareness. The 5,014-acre complex of mangrove, brush, and marsh grass has impoundments of brackish and salt water, bounded by a five-mile levee that doubles as a road.

Here an early morning drive requires only field glasses and the refuge checklist of 291 species of birds for an exercise in pure enjoyment. Snake-necked anhingas perch at the water's edge, wings held open to dry. Moorhens "geek" through the shallows. Brown pelicans weigh down the mangrove branches, and ospreys are common year-round. I left the car for a walk along a footpath, and a wood stork stalked away like a grumpy barrister.

As Darling had plenty to say about wildlife, his namesake refuge has plenty to show and several ways to see it. I tried them all, driving, walking, and canoeing a well-marked route through the mangroves in a rented craft. The calls of winged wildlife and the soft plash of the paddle are often the only sounds in this peaceful labyrinth. Young mangroves rise in twisted shapes above the surface of the crystal-clear water, and grayish mullet drift like smoke below.

Many refuges seem to have sprung full-blown from bureaucracy's head. An area is misused, abandoned, acquired by the government, sanctioned as a wildlife habitat. Not so Tijuana Slough, conceived in controversy and created amid resentment. Where the Tijuana River empties into the Pacific south of San Diego, the little city of Imperial Beach once dumped its garbage and settled its sewage. In 1959, with the fuse lit for America's recreation explosion, a land corporation bought a sizable tract and planned a marina, with other attractions. The plan was welcomed by many property owners as a boost to the economy, deplored by others as environmental rape.

"People just don't realize how much energy is created in an estuary," said red-bearded Mike McCoy, a veterinarian and vice president of the Southwest Wetlands Interpretive Association, formed to save the slough from development. "Southern California is practically back-to-back marinas up and down the coast. This is almost the last undeveloped estuary left, and habitat for two endangered species, the light-footed clapper rail and the California least tern."

The National Environmental Policy Act of 1969 and the Endangered Species Act of 1973 breathed natural life back into the slough. Ecological strictures became so complicated that the land corporation sold its tract to Fish and Wildlife. In a time of budget cuts and manpower freezes, the new refuge is being managed by officers from Salton Sea Refuge, about three hours' driving time away. Cleanup and improvement of the grounds are undertaken by local citizens on weekend work parties.

"There's still a lot of bad feeling from people who wanted a marina," said Chris McIntire of San Diego, who had worked a dozen sessions with her husband, Donovan. "One weekend we planted shrubs and the next day they were yanked out. We put up a wire fence to keep out dirt bikes and a thirty-foot section of it was cut."

A jocular gang of a dozen refuge supporters was erecting a fence of telephone poles the day I joined them. Bill Nichols, a semi-retired contractor, watched it rise near his back door. "A marina would have produced income and broadened our tax base," he said. "Imperial Beach has little else going for it."

Neighbor Tom Schaaf, mowing his lawn nearby, agreed in part. "This town is going broke. We lost our police department, and fire protection is inadequate. But a refuge is a natural resource, an education."

Jack McAfee, a naval helicopter pilot, is a realist who accepts the inevitable. He launched his stocky frame into the barricade-building. "A marina would have doubled the value of my property." He shrugged. "But this way the view will stay open. I'll learn more about birds. I'll adapt the stellar scope in my living room to a camera and get great pictures of them."

At the largest estuary of the California coast he could get all the information he needs.

"San Francisco Bay is much more geared to education than the average refuge," said its recreation planner, Michael Bitsko. "Our mission is to manage wildlife for the continuing enjoyment of people." Here schoolkids visit an education center to learn about the bay's ecology. Their teachers attend workshops on the use of the outdoors as a classroom. For other adults, other diversions. I joined a group of 17 for a hike called "The Incredible Edibles Plant Walk," on which we munched the blossoms of mustard plants and nibbled at wild radish. Our long-haired tour guide Erica Hendricks pointed out horehound and told us that the pioneers used it for cough medicine. We sampled some of her horehound candy.

Like Tijuana Slough, the bay refuge relies heavily on volunteers. "We have 51 unpaid workers who contributed $42,000 in work in 1982," said naturalist Steve Haydock. Ken Crowley, retired at 59, devotes a day a week—"I always liked the outdoors." Leading volunteer is Arthur Wellens, a United Airlines retiree who puts in 450 hours a year.

Love of wildlife creates some unlikely warriors. Mrs. Eleanor Stopps, who lives at Port Ludlow, northwest of Seattle, looks and talks like a kindly grandmother. But in the cause of Protection Island she began to scrap like a ward politician. Largely because of her efforts this chunk of land in the Strait of Juan de Fuca will become a wildlife refuge.

Protection Island, named by explorer George Vancouver in 1792, stands like a 354-acre fortress guarding an inlet called Discovery Bay. Of 29,000 pairs of seabirds nesting in the Puget Sound basin and along the strait, some 21,000 use its steep cliffs and sandy slopes. They include 17,000 pairs of rhinoceros auklets, the largest U. S. colony of that species south of Alaska.

For more than two decades, bird-lover and wildlife artist Zella Schultz sought protection for Protection. The Nature Conservancy bought 48 acres, and the State of Washington designated it the Zella M. Schultz Seabird Sanctuary in 1975, a year after her death. A group of developers decided people might like to nest on the other 306 acres. By phone calls and letters, Eleanor Stopps urged bureaucrats and congressmen to establish a national wildlife refuge.

"I was never an activist," she said as she spread the developers' plan on her kitchen countertop. "I don't even like politics, but thanks to Zella I came to care about the island as she did."

Before the refuge was authorized in 1982, 630 lots had been sold. But this retirement paradise had no water supply and no sewer system, no medical facilities, and no certain transportation to the mainland. Many buyers would be willing to sell to the government if it would meet their price. Only three families live there full-time. Still, Mrs. Stopps fears that use will increase, and disturb the birds.

Bill Hesselbart, manager of the Nisqually Refuge complex and overseer of Protection, took me there in a launch. Tufted puffins, chunky birds with sad-clown faces, skimmed off the sea ahead of us. Glaucous-winged gulls wheeled overhead, shrieking. Harbor seals humped down a beach to water and swam warily, heads held high. "It hasn't been many years since hunters shot at them," explained Hesselbart.

Once ashore, we toiled up a steep slope riddled with the nesting burrows of the rhino auklets. With beak and claws they dig ten feet or farther in sandy soil. Their little wings aid their pursuit of small fish underwater, but leave them improbable fliers. One observer described a rhino auklet coming to roost, stubby wings extended and feet braced, as looking like a falling teddy bear.

Phil Vorvick and his wife, Bonnie, comprise two-fifths of the full-time human residents. They live in the teeth of gales that can topple a tractor, and with cliff erosion that has forced them to move their house back 16 feet.

"I've been a member of Audubon Society for many years," he told me. "People like Mrs. Stopps have come on pretty strong about how we disturb the seabirds, scaring them off their nests. We've made mistakes, but to say we don't care about wildlife is not right. We don't want to see any more development, and doubt there will be any. We've told the government we want to sell to them on a 'life use' basis, meaning we can't pass the property on to heirs." A few lot-owners, he conceded, want unlimited, unending use of the land they had bought.

Phil Vorvick seems as unlikely a villain as Mrs. Stopps a fighter. The two seem unlikely antagonists, since both care about birds. Mrs. Stopps, burned by delays and witness to a decade of greed, distrusts any island resident without feathers or flippers. And Mr. Vorvick, scorched by accusations from this tigress in tennis shoes, prefers to ignore her. As happens in so many controversies, they seek similar goals from different angles and end up in deadlock.

Can coastal life and people mix, without supervision? At first glance in Hawaii, the answer would appear to be no.

"Hawaii has more endangered species than any other state," said ranger Dan Moriarty, at Kilauea Point on the island of Kauai. "There is limited habitat enclosed by ocean, heavy encroachment by man, and several introduced predators. Our biggest predators on this island are cats and dogs."

Site of an old lighthouse, Kilauea is the place to see native seabirds. They cling to and soar about the spectacular cliffs as waves churn themselves into a froth far below. The Laysan albatross rides the gusts on a wingspread of nearly six feet. Swarming like gnats around the stomach-stirring heights are white-tailed tropicbirds, both red-footed and brown boobies, and wedge-tailed shearwaters. "Dogs once killed 80 shearwaters on their nests in one night," Moriarty told me. Now a fine-mesh wire fence encloses the refuge. Even human visitors—some 350 per day—are kept out until noon to give the seabirds some time to themselves.

"We are unique in the system in that our lands are true refuges," I was told by Rob Shallenberger, youthful-looking manager of the Hawaiian and Pacific Islands Refuge complex, with headquarters in Honolulu. "We have no hunting, and in fact little public use anywhere except on Kilauea Point. The danger to species is too great."

The Hawaiian archipelago ranges over 1,500 miles, and many refuges are simply uninhabited coral atolls of a few acres, far out to sea. "If you superimposed a map of the Pacific refuges on a map of the contiguous 48 states," said assistant manager Jerry Ludwig, "Nihoa Island would be in Portland, Oregon, one reef called Pearl and

Hermes would be just north of San Diego, and Rose Atoll down in Samoa would be way northeast of Maine, somewhere in Labrador."

Was poaching a problem? I was answered by smiles. "You have to understand just how remote these islands are," said Shallenberger.

"There they are," said Ludwig above the drone of the vintage Beechcraft, four hours out of Honolulu. Ahead of us lay a scattering of white specks. The French Frigate Shoals, midway in the Hawaiian chain, are coral reefs that lie atop the remnants of an old volcano. The largest, Tern Island, was a refueling station for World War II combat planes. Nearly rectangular, with surf on the shoals at one end, it looks like an aircraft carrier in a 180-degree turn. The four caretakers living there see it more as an ark.

"We're here to make sure there's no sudden crash in population, perhaps from lost food supply," said tall, quiet Steve Fairaizl. Of the 22 seabird species in Hawaii, as many as 18 nest in French Frigate Shoals. Tern is also home to the Hawaiian monk seal, an endangered species.

"Monk seals are the most primitive of the seals," explained marine biologist Ruth Ittner, who took me on a walking tour. "They have no external ears, and they don't use their flippers to inch along on the sand as sea lions do."

They are also disappearing. Sharks? Disease? Or human presence?

"They don't seem to mind people if people don't come too close," said Ruth as we strolled within fifty feet of dozing furry lumps. "The Coast Guard ran a loran [oceanic navigation] station here for years, and we think that was disruptive. Since it closed we've seen seals increase on Tern."

When I walked down the runway a fairy tern hovered just above me like an alabaster protector. If the white tern seemed a winged saint, high above soared the sinners—prey-stealing great frigatebirds, wings bent in an M that seems to imply malevolence. There were red-tailed tropicbirds, black noddies, wedge-tailed shearwaters, and hordes of sooty terns with their constant, questioning call, "Wideawake? Wideawake? Wideawake?" Y-E-E-S-S!

My favorite was the Laysan albatross, a creature so trusting that it barely moves aside at your approach. A bluish tinge around the eye cavity gives it the look of a maiden aunt with liver trouble. Highly sociable, the birds greet each other with rituals comically human—a nodding of heads, a nibbling at beaks like two old friends bussing ("My dear, you're looking *lovely* today").

"Think I could touch one?" I asked Ruth. We stood near a female and her wobbly-necked chick on a bowl-shaped nest.

"Yes, but don't jerk your hand back when she grabs you because the hooked beak can cut."

Crouching, I moved my hand slowly forward. The bird looked this way and that in confusion and nervously popped her four-inch beak, which suddenly reached out and gently grasped my finger. Then it withdrew and I was stroking the smooth breast feathers, having to remind myself that this was a wild bird with its young. The lion and the lamb may never lie down together, but the most efficient of predators can rest next to a Laysan albatross.

They became a symbol for me, these guileless creatures, of the innocence of all wildlife, and our responsibilities to it. All evolved with skills for survival, skills virtually annulled by human misuse of them and their habitat. We need not expect to lie down with them in a miraculous peaceable kingdom, but we can at least share their world with fairness.

Multiple use on the crowded northeastern coast forces managers to segregate people from wildlife.
On Plum Island, Massachusetts, beachcombers enjoy one section of Parker River NWR while
gulls—greater black-backed and a few herring gulls (below)—keep to another. Patrols and
fences (above) at Trustom Pond Refuge in Rhode Island keep people away from the nesting areas
of least tern colonies and pairs of piping plovers. Spring sunbathers may frighten the birds
from choice sites. Later, the presence of human intruders would keep parent birds off their eggs or
away from their chicks—while hungry gulls swooped down to take this helpless prey.
Camouflage puts a plover chick (bottom) at risk from a careless human foot.

60

ALAN D. CAREY (ABOVE); JON SCHNEEBERGER, TED JOHNSON, JR., AND ANTHONY PERITORE, N.G.S. STAFF (RIGHT)

Symbols of liberty have liftoff: The space shuttle Columbia *hurtles into history on its 1981 maiden voyage; a rare southern bald eagle takes flight. NASA offered unused land near Cape Canaveral for Merritt Island Refuge, founded in 1963, home to 14 threatened or endangered species. Research shows that space-program activities, and more than two million visitors annually, have little short-term effect on wildlife; long-term effects remain unknown.*

Sportsman's whim brought exotic animals to St. Vincent Island on Florida's Gulf Coast, where a freshwater stream meanders through cattails and sawgrass. A former owner introduced African and Asian species to his private estate—a national refuge since 1968. Sambar deer from India, like the stag above, still thrive here. Key deer, natives of Florida's southern isles, faced extinction from overhunting and loss of habitat before their namesake refuge opened in 1954. Below, young visitors, heedless of "please-do-not-feed" signs, give tiny adult does a handout.

Tempest of startled Sandwich terns surrounds biologist Jake Valentine in Louisiana's Breton NWR as he estimates tern population and production by counting nests within a grid. Such studies yield scientific data and aid wildlife management. Breton's barrier islands, off the Mississippi Delta, hold large colonies of black skimmers, royal terns, and laughing gulls.

FOLLOWING PAGES: Grace unfurled, a roseate spoonbill glides above Sabine NWR in Louisiana, largest waterfowl refuge on the Gulf Coast with 139,437 acres of marsh habitat.

ERWIN AND PEGGY BAUER (FOLLOWING PAGES)

ALL BY DAVID CUPP

Sanctuary for wild things within metropolitan sprawl, San Francisco Bay NWR preserves 25 miles of shoreline on the bay. Five million people share the area with some 280 species of birds; 70 percent of shorebirds using the Pacific flyway rest or winter here. Biologist Roy W. Lowe (far left) releases a California clapper rail after banding it; concern for these endangered birds helped establish the refuge in 1974. Above, at the Environmental Education Center, local teachers study marsh plants. Walkways lead birdwatchers into a marsh. Here, says Lowe, birders now outnumber hunters.

*Three young California sea lions, scarred but safe, find a haven at Farallon NWR.
The offshore rock refuge, 30 miles west of San Francisco, shelters other pinnipeds: the
northern sea lion, harbor seal, northern fur seal, northern elephant seal. Hunters
eliminated the local elephant seals before 1850. Now, protected by law, the animals
again use the Farallons as breeding grounds, raising pups by the hundred.*

Wave-eroded Three Arch Rocks NWR lures nesting seabirds to Oregon's coast, where the federal refuge system includes isles and rocks above the mean tide line for 290 miles. On shore near Three Arch, young spruces shade white trillium and sword fern at Cape Meares NWR, where a rare stand of old-growth forest has survived uncut.

Silken sunlight of a May afternoon glosses the shallows of Grassy Island and Leadbetter Point at Willapa Refuge on Washington's southern coast. During spring and autumn migrations along the Pacific flyway, tens of thousands of birds feed and rest here—among them, the small geese called black or western brant, pausing on their long journey between Mexico and Alaska.

Wind-torn evergreen and white yarrow mark a meadow on Protection Island, Washington, a major breeding site for marine birds—saved from development by public demand in 1982. Glaucous-winged gulls, from 4,300 nesting pairs, search the bounteous sea for food. More than 17,000 pairs of rhinoceros auklets riddle the sandy cliffs with burrows as deep as 10 or 12 feet. A parent returns at night with a beakful of sand launce to feed its single nestling.

N.G.S. PHOTOGRAPHER BATES LITTLEHALES (ABOVE); PHIL VORVICK (LEFT, BELOW)

Isolated by the sea, but under the oversight of the Hawaiian and Pacific Islands Refuge complex, uninhabited isles of Pearl and Hermes Reef (opposite) and other remote atolls harbor pelagic birds such as the red-tailed tropicbird, or bosun bird (above). Threatened species of this realm include the green turtle (below, with convict tang nibbling algae on its shell); the Hawaiian monk seal, napping on a couch of sand, ranks as endangered.

PRECEDING PAGES: Gentle greeting, demure response mark the courtship of the Laysan albatross. By providing fenced nesting sites safe from predatory dogs and cats at Kilauea Point on Kauai, refuge managers in Hawaii hope to increase the local population.

THE EASTERN

Leaves touched by autumn's gold, white birches spire above their reflections in the glassy waters of a man-made marsh on Necedah NWR in central Wisconsin. Since its establishment in 1939, the refuge has reclaimed marsh, woodland, and prairie destroyed by logging, farming, and drainage. Dikes, dams, and ditches restored the marshes—one-quarter of Necedah's forty-thousand-acre habitat. Hardwood and pine trees cover more than half the refuge. Settlers felled the dense forest that once stretched from the Atlantic coast to the Mississippi River, but eastern woodlands still harbor a wide variety of wildlife.

FOLLOWING PAGES: At ease in water, a young bull moose fords a pool on northern Minnesota's Agassiz NWR. One budding antler curls upward; the other curves back toward the animal's ear.

WOODLANDS

The fire at Seney burned above ground, below ground, and deep into my understanding of wildlife refuges. As I drove toward it along Lake Superior in Michigan's Upper Peninsula, I heard radio reports that three thousand acres of federal land had been destroyed at Seney National Wildlife Refuge. Destroyed—an ominous term. Near refuge headquarters I hitched a helicopter ride with fire boss Jim Kesel, who was ferrying sandwiches and supplies to some forty fire fighters at the front lines. Sure enough, from above they seemed to stand at the dividing line between apocalypse and Eden.

At their backs were emerald seas of marsh grasses, surging wavelike in the wind, brushing against low-growing black spruce, vines of wild cranberry, and clumps of labrador tea. Where wind ages ago had pushed up sand ridges a few feet high, red and jack pine clustered in mini-forests.

Before them lay the black blankness that only fire can wreak. Most of the flames had been extinguished, but grass and bushes were seared to the ground in their wake. Where peat in the marsh soil had ignited, it smoldered a foot or so below the surface, and smoke hung everywhere in a pungent fog.

Leaders of the fire-fighting effort were unexpectedly calm, despite some concern that flames might stray onto private property. On a wildlife refuge, fire is more often a tool than a terror.

"It almost always improves the habitat," shouted Kesel above the *whop-whop-whop* of the helicopter blades. "It knocks back brush and maintains open areas for deer and bear. It creates nesting grounds for ruffed grouse and sandhill cranes. The yellow rails—that's a species in trouble—the rails will love it."

He pressed his forehead against the chopper bubble to survey the blackness below: "This will all be green by next spring."

"This is not a disaster," refuge manager Don Frickie told me later. "It may have been started by lightning, but we start many fires ourselves—what we call prescribed burning." Destruction, it appears, is in the eye of the beholder.

When the colonists pushed inland from the Atlantic seaboard, they entered a seemingly unending forest. A squirrel hopping from branch to branch, it's said, could have traveled from Jamestown to the Mississippi and never touched ground. The trees were cut for construction, fields cleared for agriculture. Michigan's towering white pines—nearly all of them felled by the turn of the century—helped rebuild Chicago after the great fire of 1871. Today the state ranks 16th in agricultural acreage: food and homes for people at the expense of wildlife.

That presettlement world is not accurately re-created by simply drawing a boundary around an area and announcing hands off to development. Woods are lovely, dark and deep, as Robert Frost's poem reminds us, but they are also dynamic. Fire, it is now believed, has played an important part in cycles of regrowth. Lightning could touch off a fire; Indians could set it. "This area has been burned over many times in the past," said Leon Guzinski, fire supervisor for Michigan's Department of Natural Resources and a consultant at the Seney fire.

After the fire was contained, Don Frickie, a hulking, red-bearded man whose overhanging brows give him a look of Job-like patience, insisted on showing me the unburned parts of the 95,000-acre refuge—"one of the prettiest in the system." I'd heard that line before, elsewhere, but Seney pleaded its case well.

Scattered about the refuge and connected by grit roads are 21 sky-blue pools lined with conifers. Dotting the pools are small grassy islands where Canada geese lay their eggs. The ponds, the islands, even the presence of geese are the work of the refuge system. "By 1935 this area was being called a desert," Don said. " The pine ridges had been logged and fires had burned out many of the bogs. Geese that had nested here went elsewhere."

The ravaged land was acquired by the federal government, and the ponds were built by the CCC, the Civilian Conservation Corps. Canada geese were brought here and their wings clipped to assure a temporary stay so their goslings would become imprinted on the refuge. The flock that now returns produces about 300 new geese each spring. In fall they wing off with their parents to the wintering ranges of the South. One of these, like Seney, was created from land badly scarred by peaceful misuse. It is managed by a man badly scarred by war.

On a cool January day near Decatur, Alabama, Tom Atkeson takes me on an automobile tour of Wheeler Refuge. We are driving through farm fields much of the time. Wheeler was a pioneer in raising crops for wildlife on a cooperative basis with local farmers, who take three-fourths of the harvest and leave a fourth for waterfowl.

"This cornfield was picked clean when I checked it last week," says the manager as the dark heads of Canada geese watch us warily a quarter mile away. "There might be a little feed left at this end . . . Carolyn, do you see any?"

Carolyn Garrett, a handsome, ebullient woman in her 40s, is driving the car. Outdoor recreation planner for the refuge, she sometimes lends a hand—and eyesight—to Tom Atkeson, who has neither. An antitank mine blew up in his face while he was defusing it during World War II, an incident he describes casually as "getting tattered and torn during the unpleasantries." The refuge and its manager are both studies in understatement.

"I came to work as a biologist in 1939," explains Atkeson. "The land had been shaved off for farming, used up; and it was eroding badly. We built check dams, planted trees, and established good cropping practices. This is a refuge where habitat is highly artificial, man-made."

In 1939, 1,500 ducks found the new winter haven. The first geese arrived in 1941, about the time Japanese bombers attacked Pearl Harbor and Tom Atkeson went off to war. There's been a lot of healing by the man and the refuge since then.

For 45 years this tall, thin, energetic man has worked on the refuge; he has managed it for half that time. His eyes burn with intensity, like the blue light thrown from a hidden welder's torch. How does one manage a 13-employee facility of 34,119 acres that one can neither see nor touch?

"I mapped the refuge in the years before the war, so it is a picture I never forgot," he tells me. "I know every inch. When Carolyn drives I can tell how fast we're going and I recognize bumps and bridges."

" Tom," says Carolyn as we drive a road that winds through partially wooded bottomland, "people have been throwing a lot of trash on the left side here. Should we get somebody out here to pick it up, and maybe put up some signs?"

"Well, you're off refuge land now, Carolyn."

"Oh right, I am."

Wounds to earth are seldom more grievous than those inflicted on the Georgia Piedmont. There, white settlers of the late 18th and early 19th centuries leveled forests and turned the loamy topsoil to grow cotton. The skin of the earth sloughed off, washed downstream, leaving the land red and raw and, in a rainstorm, bleeding. With the soil's vitality sapped, many farmers moved on to more fertile ground.

In the late 1930s the Bureau of Biological Survey acquired 30,000 acres to create a national wildlife refuge. A regional supervisor wrote in a memorandum that if wildlife could be restored to Piedmont Refuge it could surely be restored anywhere.

On the rolling hills deer are now so plentiful that hunters harvest about 600 a year, and also take squirrels, rabbits, and quail. The flourishing of wildlife is due in large part to the harvest of trees. The timbering techniques draw observers from all over the world.

"Lots of animals use the edge of two habitats, wooded and clear," said assistant manager Mark Musaus as we drove through stands of loblolly pine, or mixed groves of oak and hickory. "We create edge habitat by the way we cut, which also speeds the growth of trees."

Piedmont is divided into 35 compartments of 1,000 acres apiece. Within each compartment, the pines are cut in plots so that all levels of growth are represented. During growth they are thinned several times, with underbrush burned off.

Refuge forester Dave Heiges explained: "We like to show the private landowner that good timber management can be good wildlife management. If he thins a dense pine stand by cutting pulpwood it will help tree growth—and give him an early income. In the meantime, he's also benefiting wildlife by allowing more sunlight to reach the forest floor to stimulate herbaceous growth."

Nothing demonstrates the success of the Piedmont program better than the survival of the red-cockaded woodpecker, which requires tall, mature trees with special features. The modern timber industry is not known for letting trees grow to full maturity. Piedmont makes it a point to leave quite a few in each compartment. Most hole-drilling birds select dead trees; but the red-cockaded attacks the living pine in which so-called red-heart disease, a fungus infection, has softened the heartwood. Red heart develops in trees more than half a century old.

I found such a tree where a young male was carving a hole to start a new colony. As he disappeared inside to excavate I would advance a few steps, then freeze when he popped out again. As in a children's game of "red light, green light," I moved and froze, moved and froze, sweat trickling down my back in the August heat when he emerged to kick out shavings and check for intruders. Finally I stood close enough to hear the tiny peck, peck, peck of his bill against solid heartwood, a faint sound of unalterable determination.

Far north of Georgia, on the Maine-New Brunswick border, Moosehorn Refuge practices similar forestry for a slightly different purpose. Sectional cutting of timber in this area of rich greenery creates young-forest habitat preferred by moose, deer, and ruffed grouse, but Moosehorn is particularly interested in its effect on a bird that weighs only eight ounces or less.

The American woodcock has a long bill that probes the ground efficiently in search of earthworms. Moreover, the upper mandible has a unique tip, flexible and sensitive; this tip feels the prey and opens to grasp it so it can be pulled to the surface and devoured. The bird's eyes are set high on the head, allowing a perfect view above and around it, for the woodcock is a devoted practitioner of the art of camouflage. If alarmed, it freezes. If flushed, it resorts to a zigzag flight through the trees that makes it a difficult—and popular—target for hunters. It's not prized for its taste. The constant diet of worms gives it a strong flavor that few humans relish.

Its range extends from Maine to Florida, and into the Midwest; along the Atlantic flyway its numbers are declining. Hunting doesn't account for its plight.

Into the Maine woods I went one day in May with Patuxent biologist Eric Derleth, who is assisting in a telemetry study of its survival and movement patterns in spring and summer. Eric wore earphones, carried a radio receiver over his shoulder, and extended an antenna before him like a divining rod.

"The hens are very successful in raising broods to flying age, but something happens to them after that," he said as we crunched through the previous fall's dead leaves. "We're trying to pinpoint their daily movements to find out what. We'd like to know what percentage of young survive their first summer of life."

The pinging radio signal in his headset led him within yards of a hen carrying a four-gram transmitter on her back. He edged in carefully, studied the ground, and said, " There she is." He was pointing almost at our feet. The ground cover was not heavy—a few sprigs of sarsaparilla, trillium, ferns, and starflowers—but still I looked for half a minute before making out the dark head with streaks like dappled sunlight, two dark eyes, and a bird unmoving as a stone.

In early evening I accompanied college-age volunteers who set up mist nets to catch woodcocks and emplace more transmitters. I drifted away to an area of forest regrowth where refuge biologist Greg Sepik said a male woodcock might be appealing for a mate. In the romantic extravagance of its aerial poetry, the chunky little bird is a feathered Lord Byron, a winged Keats.

On the ground fifty yards away I heard a metallic *peent,* best said while holding one's nose. Then with a whistle of wind through his primary feathers he climbed until he was a dot against the evening sky. Within view of any nearby hen he swooped and darted in tight circles while sending down the most amorous trilling I've ever heard. As a crowning show-off maneuver he folded his wings and dropped like a rock, opening them again at the last instant and swooping back to his bower, where I had crept close during the blindness of his ardor.

"*Peent,*" he called hopefully. "*Peent.*"

No hen came. He began strutting up and down the little barren space, then saw me and froze. Embarrassed, as though I had been spying on a teenager primping before a mirror, I crept away and rejoined the mist-net crew.

Some refuges are praised for providing food that attracts wildlife. Others are blamed. Southern hunters have accused northern refuges of creating such plentiful food supplies that Canada geese cut short their southward migration—a practice known as "short-stopping." Deliberate short-stopping is against Fish and Wildlife policy, but many Southerners believe it continues, covertly. "Let me put it this way," said a refuge manager far below the Mason-Dixon line. "If a large number of geese hang around your refuge it looks like you're a good manager."

Nearly 148,000 geese have been counted on Montezuma Refuge in the New York Finger Lakes region during spring and fall migrations. Surprisingly, some 60,000 spend the winter.

Does that make manager Grady Hocutt a short-stopper?

"Not at all," the former college instructor answered cheerfully. "Geese stay here because farmers have doubled the corn harvest since 1975 and the birds feed on dropped grain. They have food, and open water at Cayuga Lake nearby—two things that keep geese from moving south. And now, whole generations of them have lost the tradition of going south. I wish they would. We could lose thousands to stress-caused diseases some winter if we get a wet snow followed by a sweep of polar air."

Away from the large impoundments I skirted small marshy ponds where local teachers, trained by refuge officers, bring pupils to discover the world beneath the surface. "You can dip a net in there and come up with a whole community under the microscope," Hocutt told me later. "The kids love it."

In one recent year at Montezuma nearly 5,000 students saw presentations about refuge development and operations. Sometimes the kids give inspiration in return. In 1982 four fifth-grade students used money earned in the sale of pencils, paper, and erasers to buy and build two osprey nesting platforms.

Grady Hocutt tells of the donation with pride as we drive the dike of the largest impoundment, nearly covered by Canada geese. They lumber off the water like jumbo jets, lifting in a gray cloud, filling the air with a cascade of honking. Hocutt stops the car and rolls down the window to watch and listen. "When I get tired of that I'll start screwing nuts on bolts for a living," he says.

Geese, particularly the big Canadas and the lovely snows, capture the human imagination like no other wild game bird. Perhaps, as Frankie Laine sang in the 1950s, the seasonal flights in the familiar V's symbolize a victory over a fettered existence.

"My heart knows what the wild goose knows / And I must go where the wild goose goes, / Wild goose, brother goose, which is best, / A wand'rin' foot or a heart at rest?"

"Their large size is attractive to people, but to those who really know them, so is their behavior," says Dr. Donald Rusch, a biologist at the University of Wisconsin at Madison, who has studied geese for years. "They're very sociable, they mate for life, and the goose family is the basic social unit. People see some parallels to their own life in that."

Most of Dr. Rusch's studies have been done on glacier-gouged Horicon Marsh, an hour's drive northeast of Madison. Every fall the huge flocks of Canadas in the wetlands of Horicon Wildlife Refuge draw thousands of people from Madison, Milwaukee, and Chicago. Cars jam State Route 49, which crosses an area where the birds congregate. The spectacle pleases orchard owner Gerald Gruhn, for the goose-watchers generally clean out his fall crop of apples. Other farmers are less happy, for the geese can clean out theirs: corn and winter wheat.

When goose concentrations exceeded 200,000 birds, cries of short-stopping were heard from the south and farmers near the marsh appealed to their congressmen. In 1976 a hazing program was undertaken, to scatter the birds and hasten migration. Flocks that settled on Horicon waters were buzzed by airboats; farmers were given propane "scareaway guns" that went off in the fields every five minutes, and area hunting quotas were increased. The annual goose visitation was halved.

"They could decimate a field before the hazing," farmer Gary Jesse told me. "If I hadn't patrolled my fields and fired my propane guns we could have lost 90 percent of the corn." Still, he added, "I enjoy having them here as long as their numbers are reasonable. If I lose about 100 bushels of corn a year that's all right. I'm willing to do my share in feeding the wildlife."

The appetite of another species creates a double benefit. Muskrats eat cattail roots and help maintain open water for waterfowl nesting and feeding, and trappers bid thousands of dollars yearly for the right to catch the furbearers. Those over 65 or under 18 may trap an assigned area gratis.

Full of energy, tightly muscled, a red foxtail dangling from the back of his duck-hunting cap, 19-year-old Chris Manninen would fit right in at a rendezvous of 19th-century mountain men. In the winter of 1982-83 his catch of more than 1,400 'rats, 16 raccoons, and 5 mink brought more than $5,000—not bad for a high school senior. He bought 40 female and 8 male mink to begin a fur ranch. "Dad wants me to go to college," he told me, "but if I can make it trapping and raising mink—well, I just love it on Horicon Marsh."

In wetlands or woodlands, man can unmake in decades what nature had built over thousands of years. Hardwood swamps once covered 2,500,000 acres of what is now Missouri. Of those, only 50,000 remain undrained and uncut in the southeast part of the state, and nearly half are within Mingo Refuge. Even that has required restoration. When Herman Wilfong was growing up here, "smoke hung over the area all winter from people burning piles of wood from trees cleared for farming."

Judge Wilfong, as he's called, has hunted the "bootheel" area for half a century; he grazed cattle in the swamp near Puxico when it was still a hunter's paradise. "When the ducks and geese came in to feed they would just darken the sun," he told me. Turkeys roamed the oak-and-hickory forest on higher ground. . . .

Head bobbing, red wattles swinging with each step, the big tom moved slowly through the spring dawn. Occasionally he emitted a shrill gobble that carried a mile. The sun was gleaming off his iridescent feathers when he was answered by the higher-pitched call of a hen. He headed for the sound, gobbling encouragement, receiving some in return. At last she seemed quite close, perhaps among the fading leaves of that windblown oak, but . . . something was wrong. The hen had not shown herself, and at close range her calls seemed strained and different. He paused, then began edging away. Something moved under the tree. The tom quickened his steps, his brain flashing signals to his wings, when a fierce wind came and blew him into darkness.

"He weighed a little over 20 pounds," said Judge Wilfong, who related his version of that turkey's last day to me.

Hunting aside, Mingo offers softer echoes to a primeval past. A mile-long boardwalk allows a dry-footed stroll over a quagmire heavy with the scent of lush greenery and alive with birds, more than 200 species. In spring the "bluff trail" is a walk through a riot of wildflowers—redbud, bluebells, Dutchman's-breeches like little baggy trousers upside down, bloodroot that Indians used to make red dye.

"Swamps are neat," said young Tom Bell, an assistant manager, as we walked a dripping path. "Lots of people think of them in the context of some grade B horror movie until they see how alive they are. We get a lot of repeat visitors."

Shooting stars, columbine, jack-in-the-pulpit, wild sweet william, spring beauty, six kinds of blue violets—Mingo is a charmer.

But if you like your swamps served up with a touch of mystery, a dash of suspense, and a spontaneous shiver, Okefenokee may be your ideal. Who can't find mystery in netherworld shapes of cypress knees, and the Spanish moss that hangs like cobwebs and faded lace in a Gothic mansion? There's a twinge of suspense in knowing that by carelessness you can get lost in 429,000 acres, more than nine-tenths of it wildlife refuge. And the shiver? Mine came nine miles deep in the swamp at an isolated camp on high ground called Cravens (as in coward) Hammock. More about that later.

A quarter of a million visitors entered America's best-known swamp in 1983. Especially popular are 13 canoe trails, used by some 5,000 paddlers annually. The total is small because canoe parties go at intervals, separated for a sense of solitude.

"Some get lost when they try to explore off the marked trail," said refuge manager John Schroer. "Some have been stranded overnight, but we've never lost anyone permanently."

With my wife, Barbara Payne, researcher on this book and my companion at several refuges, I rented a canoe and set off on the Brown Trail, an overnight voyage. The day was bright, the paddling pleasantly strenuous. Not until we turned off the open water of Billys Lake, following the white blazes of the trail, did we realize that the Okefenokee would make us work for her pleasures.

The route narrowed to a grass-lined passage. We reached our first clump of lilies, a paddling purgatory. White water lilies blanketed the surface; the taller yellow spatterdock reached above the gunwales. No more stroke and glide, stroke and glide.

The plants muttered against the hull and tangled on our paddles as we pushed forward foot by foot, as though levering through a cabbage patch. Minutes dragged by and the sun beat down in the still air. Just as minds and muscles turned numb with monotony, Barbara in the bow would announce breathlessly, "They're beginning to thin out," and we would surge again into blessed glassy water.

Great blue herons rowed the air overhead, toes pointed like ballet dancers'. Sandhill cranes flushed from brushy shores, uttering their low flutelike calls. Vultures drew lazy circles overhead, and smaller birds—warblers, woodpeckers, thrushes—flitted in and out of underbrush. And always there were alligators.

Strange, our fascination with these expressionless creatures. Do they represent, along with the steamy richness of the swamp, a sense of gazing back into the dawn of life? Most of them slid beneath the surface well ahead of us, but a few large ones, content on logs in the sun, refused to budge as we glided by within five yards. Our count had passed two dozen and been abandoned by the time we eased onto Cravens Hammock in late afternoon and set up camp in a small clearing.

Next morning we heard a noise that made coffee cups pause halfway to our mouths. It was a growl, starting low and crescendoing before trailing off again.

"Sounds like a bear," I said. "It'll leave as soon as it knows we're here." I picked up a paddle, banged on the canoe, and yelled, but the growls continued, louder now and from two directions! Apprehension flared until logic caught up. We were hearing the morning mutter of two bull alligators.

It was our only moment of unease in this beautiful place. The mystery and the suspense had been everything we had expected, and less. Thanks to the gators, we even had a little shiver. No first-time swamper should be without it.

The distant growl of traffic might be a more likely sound at Minnesota Valley, where a refuge is being carved from river floodplain near the urban hubbub of Minneapolis-St. Paul. Ducks dabble in the cooling pond of a power plant or dive in the cleaned-up water of a sewage-treatment lagoon, while airliners wing low on final approach to the international airport.

Along the Minnesota River for 36 miles the new complex winds in snakelike shape, a patchwork of federal, state, and private lands. It now protects 10,000 acres; 18,000 is the target figure, most of this within the city limits of nine suburban communities and easily accessible to two million residents.

"People here were fed up with landfills and garbage dumps," said Ed Crozier, manager of the developing refuge. "Now we have strong public support."

"When we first tried to create a refuge the Department of the Interior turned us down," I was told by Elaine Mellott, chairman of Friends of the Minnesota Valley, Inc. "No money available. But support has come in from about 45 organizations—city councils, conservation groups, and industry. Minnesota has a reverence for wildlife that I don't think is present in many other states."

Congress provided money in 1976. The results include not only habitat for wildlife but also a growing complex of horse trails, observation blinds, hiking paths, and cross-country ski routes. Citizens still take part in some phases of refuge work.

Early one June morning I joined volunteers Kate Crowley, Kay Schwie, and Jane Pettit as they strolled a mile of tree-lined riverfront for a monthly bird count. The figures go into a computer, to be monitored for any fluctuations in populations. Armed with binoculars, field guides, and checklists, the three identified winged residents by sight and song: three house wrens, a great crested flycatcher, two yellow warblers, three goldfinches, a red-eyed vireo. The list grew.

"We notice changes," said Kate Crowley. "FWS quit planting millet and sunflower seeds on a field one year, and the sparrow count went down that winter." A flash of wings brought the glasses back to her eyes: "American redstart, two."

Also mourning dove, pewee, three more goldfinches, and . . . hark to the sound of the warbling vireo, which trills something like "If I see you I will seize you and I'll squeeze you till you squirt." Or so say the birders.

I took to the air for another bird count in Minnesota, at a refuge where the eastern woodlands meet the midwestern prairies. Pilot/biologist John Winship met me at the Minneapolis airport late in March for a low-level ride in his push-pull plane, a Cessna Skymaster with props fore and aft.

"If you're surveying at 100 feet and one engine goes out, you can pull out of it with no loss of stability or altitude," he explained.

"What you up to today, John?" asked the woman behind the hangar counter.

"Counting eagles."

" Shouldn't take you long. Aren't many left around here, are there?"

"About 200 nesting pairs in Minnesota. About that many in Wisconsin."

"Really! I thought they were endangered!"

Good news sometimes brightens the often-depressing statistics on wildlife. The ban on DDT, steep fines for killing the birds, and a program of translocating captive hatchlings have resulted in a comforting increase in our national bird.

We headed for Tamarac Wildlife Refuge in northwestern Minnesota, named—with a variant spelling—for a conifer that loses its needles in winter and stands like the ghost of a Christmas tree past. "Three years ago there were only two active nests at Tamarac, and last year there were nine," said Winship. The ride grew bumpy. The wind was gusting to 30 miles per hour when we picked up Tamarac manager Omer Swenson at a small airport near the refuge.

From the air, Tamarac's unspoiled aspect is unmistakable. Most of the 42,725 acres have never felt a plow, and the 21 major lakes offer a smorgasbord of fish for the eagles that nest on their wooded shores. The nests encumber the highest pines— masses of sticks, four to six feet wide and several feet thick, a fine vantage point for eagles and a boon to eagle counters as well.

We swooped around the lakeshores, noting pairs of eggs on some nests, incubating birds on others. The plane wobbled and fishtailed. Treetops came within 200 feet of us: white pine, black spruce, aspen, ash, bur oak, elm. In wing-standing turns Winship made quick adjustments to the controls as gusts tried to flip us upside down. "Main thing to remember is to keep up your airspeed," he said lazily.

The majestic eagles showed no alarm at our roaring presence. Those on the nests simply glared like caretakers at a nursery, and soaring birds craned their necks as if to say, "Humph, just another big show-off and a rather loud one at that."

Human activity on the ground is another story, for eagles will tolerate little of it during the nesting season. "Logging companies now cooperate by leaving at least ten acres around an eagle nest," Swenson told me.

We spotted eight active nests, a slight variation from the previous year but of little concern. "We used to find several birds every year that had been shot, before the alarm was raised that they might become extinct," he said. "With tougher enforcement and nationwide concern, the eagle's on its way back."

In 1983, the Wisconsin count had 252 young; Minnesota, 321.

"Of course," Swenson concluded, "cooperation was easier to come by because it is the national bird. But if you provide the habitat and intelligent protection for any species, the animals will usually take care of themselves."

Crazy quilt of islands, sandbars, marshes, and water, the Upper Mississippi River Wildlife and Fish Refuge hugs the river for 284 miles through Minnesota, Wisconsin, Iowa, and Illinois. Millions of waterfowl migrate through it on the Mississippi flyway. Erosion from farmlands, barge traffic, and recreational use threaten the diverse refuge habitats. A ring-necked duck and her brood on Agassiz NWR will follow the Mississippi south for the winter.

Food for man and
beast abounds as it
has for centuries in
the bogs of Tamarac
NWR in Minnesota,
where Chippewas use
age-old methods to
harvest wild rice. One
Indian poles the
canoe; the other bends
rice stalks over and
taps the heads so that
ripe kernels fall into
the boat. The
northern half of
Tamarac lies within
the White Earth
Indian Reservation.
White Earth
Chippewas have
priority rights to
trapping and ricing
on the refuge; the rice
also sustains
migrating ducks
and geese.

Bleached snags, remains of the original forest, stud a 1,300-acre impoundment edged by farm fields on New York's Montezuma NWR; cattails mat the surface. Until landowners began to drain it in 1907, the Montezuma Marsh in the heart of the Finger Lakes region covered more than 75 square miles. Since 1937 the refuge has reflooded old wetlands for visiting, feeding, and nesting waterfowl. Muskrats, woodchucks, and deer inhabit the swamp woodland, upland forest, and fields; crab apples in an overgrown tract (left) tempt whitetails and ruffed grouse.

Wired for sound, biologist Eric Derleth tracks American woodcocks fitted with radio transmitters in a study of the birds on Moosehorn NWR in Maine. The refuge cuts timber to provide the young second-growth hardwood stands woodcocks need; above, Youth Conservation Corps workers clear a strip. Male woodcocks display and court in clearings; as trees return, the birds nest and feed in early growth. During the day woodcocks, which blend into the forest floor, rest and feed in dense cover.

Graceful squad of tundra swans flies in formation over Mattamuskeet NWR in eastern North Carolina. The birds, which travel almost 4,000 miles from nesting grounds in the Canadian Arctic and Alaska, feed and rest on freshwater Lake Mattamuskeet. Below, lined up like targets in a shooting gallery, American coots paddle the 42,000-acre expanse. Hundreds of tundra swans bob in the mist beyond bald cypresses. Thirty thousand of these birds (formerly called whistling swans), geese, ducks, and coots winter on Mattamuskeet, the largest natural lake in North Carolina.

FOLLOWING PAGES: Fishermen share the cypress-draped shallows of Reelfoot NWR in northwest Tennessee and southwest Kentucky with waterfowl, wintering bald eagles, and migrating songbirds. In 1811-1812 earthquakes sank dozens of square miles of swampy Tennessee woodlands; creeks and streams flooded the depression, creating Reelfoot. Locally designed boats, "stump-jumpers," slip safely over submerged logs in the 14,500-acre lake.

Clinging to her nest cavity in a longleaf pine, a red-cockaded woodpecker tends her young on Carolina Sandhills NWR in South Carolina. Once found from Maryland to Texas, red-cockadeds—now endangered—struggle to survive as timbering reduces their habitat. Unlike other woodpeckers, these nest in living trees. They prefer old pines, usually more than 70 years of age, and ease their work by attacking trees infected with a heartrot fungus that softens the wood. Pecking out a cavity may take several years, and only one bird roosts in each hole at any time. Red-cockadeds, which live in clans of two to nine birds with one breeding pair, may forage over several hundred acres of mature pine forest. Foresters harvest young pines; fewer trees live to meet the specific needs of the red-cockaded woodpecker. Carolina Sandhills supports at least 130 colonies on its 45,591 acres—more than any other national wildlife refuge. Below, at Georgia's Piedmont NWR, which holds about 30 colonies, commercial logger Thomas Jackson thins a 40-year-old stand of loblolly pines to open the area and speed growth; he works by refuge guidelines.

DAVID CUPP (ABOVE); N.G.S. PHOTOGRAPHER BATES LITTLEHALES (OPPOSITE)

Narrow route in a watery realm of dense marsh, islands, and forested swamp, a boat trail etches a dark line on the Okefenokee NWR in southeastern Georgia and northern Florida. The refuge covers 90 percent of the Okefenokee Swamp, a saucer-shaped peat bog stretching 660 square miles. Visitors tour the swamp in canoes or small motorized boats (top). Alligators bask among water lilies near the trails; more than 10,000 of the reptiles, one of the largest populations in the United States, flourish on the refuge.

Cordgrass marsh mirrors sunset and cabbage palms at Florida's Lake Woodruff NWR. Shreds of eggshell crown a white ibis hatching in an Okefenokee rookery. Like the Okefenokee, best seen by boat, Lake Woodruff contains 18,400 acres of freshwater wetlands, hardwood swamps, and pinelands, where ibises and herons perch near bald eagles, alligators, and manatees. At Lake Woodruff, established for migratory birds in 1964, piedmont and subtropical vegetation merge. Woods from the eastern coasts to the central prairies—birch, aspen, cypress, pine and palm—offer shelter, safety, and sustenance to wildlife as diverse as the trees themselves.

WENDELL METZEN (ABOVE); N.G.S. PHOTOGRAPHER BATES LITTLEHALES (OPPOSITE)

THE PRAIRIES

Wintering mallards rocket from a cattail-rimmed marsh on Quivira National Wildlife Refuge in Kansas. In the heartland of the continent, a million square miles of grassland once supported a rich fauna; pools and marshes provided food, cover, and resting places for migratory waterfowl. Then settlers plowed the prairie and drained the wetlands. The federal government preserves and manages fragments of prairie for wildlife today. Quivira, created in 1955, protects 21,820 acres of marsh and grassland.

FOLLOWING PAGES: *On a flooded mud flat at Bowdoin NWR in northeastern Montana, an American avocet feigns a broken wing to distract an intruder near its young.*

The glow in the east turns pink. Fingers of mauve reach halfway across the sky, and the growing light renders every protruding object in the blackest ink. Dawn on the plains is a world of silhouettes, many of them relatively new. An oil pump nods, a windmill spins lazily, cottonwood trees lean and whisper among themselves. As the light grows stronger, vireos, chickadees, and scissor-tailed flycatchers make announcements. That too is new.

Charles Darling, lanky and kinked forward slightly at the waist, strolls to the flagpole to raise the colors over Quivira National Wildlife Refuge near Stafford, Kansas. "You a hunter?" he asks a trifle churlishly as I approach.

"Nope, just doing a little birding." At this early hour it appears neither of us is ready to start the day's business. Inside the small brick headquarters, cups of coffee warm the atmosphere. Charles Darling, incidentally, is not related to "Ding."

"A hundred years ago there were very few songbirds here," says Darling. "Mostly meadowlarks. And bobwhite quail. There were very few trees, you see. Then homesteaders found that under the Timber Culture Act of 1873 they could get an extra quarter section of land if they started a woodlot, so they would get cottonwood limbs from Medicine Lodge in spring and stick them in the ground. The CCC started shelterbelts in the '30s to stop the dirt from blowing, so what had been grassland became spotted with trees. With the trees came the birds."

With the homesteaders had come the plow and the windmill, for croplands and livestock grazing. With the towns came automobiles and a thirst for petroleum. There were half a dozen oil wells pumping on Quivira's 21,820 acres when Charles Darling took over as manager in 1966. Now there are 22, and exploration continues.

Mountains, forests, and coastlines tend to seize the romantic consciousness of Americans. Before settlement, however, "the land between" held the biggest concentrations of America's wildlife. The waving seas of grass fed massive herds of bison and pronghorn, and hosts of smaller mammals and reptiles. Wolves culled the weaker large animals; coyotes gnawed the remains and preyed on smaller game. Prairie dog towns miles long fed hawks, owls, snakes, and ferrets.

"Quivira" meant a land of fabulous gold and silver to Coronado, who came north from Mexico seeking it—in vain—in 1541. The explorer passed not far from the refuge's two marshes, made brackish by saline groundwater, that lie near the center of Kansas and nearly at the center of the contiguous 48 states. In fall white pelicans wheel overhead, and in spring snowy plovers and least terns nest on the mud flats. Ducks and geese, once hunted by the Wichita Indians, are now hunted by anyone with a shotgun and a Kansas license.

In many other ways the prairie has changed, perhaps more dramatically than the woodlands. The seas of grass in Kansas have been turned and planted in wheat, sorghum, and hay crops. Trees have appeared where there were none. The songbirds came, and the buffalo went away. . . .

"Boys, let's remember one thing about herding these animals," said Bob Ellis to the dozen riders seated around the table at another refuge headquarters. "You can drive a buffalo anywhere *it* wants to go."

It was April, early enough for winter to shuck out more snow in Nebraska—which it did—and late enough to move the bison herd at Fort Niobrara Wildlife Refuge to richer pastures. The 225 woolly-humped bovines had wintered in erosion-cut canyons on the north bank of the Niobrara River. There they found protection from the wind, as well as spring-fed streams, and pockets of grass to sustain them through the cold months without human care.

"These are remnants of the original plains buffalo, heavier than some of the

European bison that have been kept elsewhere," the lean, energetic, whip-cracking refuge manager told me later. "Some of our bulls will go 2,000 pounds."

But, he reminded his riders, "they're agile, more agile than a horse. So drive them hard but never too close, 'cause they'll turn on you. And don't push your horses early; they may need their speed to get away in a pinch."

A late winter blow moaned above us when we saddled up. As a newcomer to the drive, I was assigned to stick with Ellis, who was on a fine-limbed Arabian stallion, a ballet dancer of a horse. Mine was a stubby, no-nonsense borrowed cow pony named Socks, who'd never seen a buffalo. When he did, his ears shot up and his nostrils flared briefly as if he were thinking *what in Secretariat's name are those critters, the ugliest cows I've ever seen.* But soon he set to herding bison with a veteran's nonchalance—a real blue-collar cayuse.

The buffalo lived up to their reputations for agility, pouring like thick chocolate over the steep slope called "the cliff" and racing away unscathed at the bottom. It was a bit later when they proved their singlemindedness.

Jim Matthews, a regional supervisor who had come from Denver for the roundup, and I were sent ahead to move the main herd along while other riders flushed stragglers from hiding places. We rode at the dark mass on a hilltop, confidently, yelling our *hy-a-a-ahs* and waving our arms. They looked at us—two riders—and turned and came disdainfully toward us, a few bulls at first and then the whole bunch. "Let's get out of here!" yelled Matthews, and we galloped in retreat until the animals lost interest. It took two more riders, including Ellis with his popping whip, to get them on the move and out the gate and on toward the south pasture.

Though the bison could be difficult, it was a pair of longhorn steers that nearly buffaloed us. Seven had wintered with the buffs, but the drive had produced only five. A half dozen of us found the last two in a wild plum thicket, and they led us on a fox-and-goose chase that went on for hours. The lean, muscular animals with the wide-span horns sneaked in and out of thickets, trotted up and down narrow canyons. Socks gamely plunged up one steep embankment after another to find them, his muzzle nearly touching the ground, and his ribs heaved beneath me as he thundered down draws to head off their efforts at doubling back.

They seemed wily as coyotes, rangy as deer, and more at home in the brush than in a pasture. Why was a wildlife refuge keeping cattle? I found out in detail months later on sunbaked plains two states away.

Granitic islands in a flatland sea, the Wichita Mountains bulged upward 300 million years ago halfway between the present-day Rockies and the Appalachians. The tallest is less than 2,500 feet. It is a mind-soothing landscape of boulder-strewn mountains and rolling plains, sought out by one and a quarter million visitors a year. Much of the 60-by-25-mile range is within the Wichita Mountains Wildlife Refuge in southwestern Oklahoma.

"We're more people-oriented than most refuges, but of course our primary job is managing wildlife," said the boyish-faced manager, Bob Karges, as he showed me a new campground complete with tent sites, group shelters, and electrical hookups for 23 trailers. A hot shower and television in your mobile home may be only minutes away from vistas of the Old West—bison and longhorns grazing on prairie grass.

The buffalo had plummeted from an estimated 60 million to near extinction by 1907, when 15 survivors at the New York Zoo were crated and sent to the Wichitas. The herd of 600 now roaming within the fences of the 92-square-mile refuge exceeds the total number of buffalo in the United States at the turn of the century. Once wild, free-roaming creatures, they learned to live with fences. For the longhorns, the reverse was true.

After the Texas revolution of 1836, many departing Mexican ranchers simply abandoned their herds, descended from Spanish stock but mixed with Mexican "common cattle" and the cows of American settlers. By the end of the Civil War an estimated three and a half million of these "wild cattle" were wandering about the brushlands of Texas. With the demand for red meat growing in the East, it became profitable to round them up and herd them to Kansas railheads.

The legend of the trail-driving cowboy has never died out, but the fierce longhorns nearly did. By the 1920s they were all but gone, crossbred with and replaced by tamer, bulkier cattle. A search was launched for animals best fitting the longhorn description: slab-sided, sway-backed, wild-eyed and long-faced with coarse hair about the head and ears. Thirty were selected and moved to the refuge in 1927.

There, like the buffalo, they have lived off the land. "All we provide is a trace mineral salt that is missing here," said Karges. "All we do medically is vaccinate them for brucellosis. Oklahoma law requires that now. Through natural selection in the wild these cattle are not very susceptible to disease."

Their hardiness and other merits have not gone unnoticed by modern cattlemen. An annual September sale to keep the herd at manageable size draws breeders from several states. Colorado rancher Darol Dickinson gave me a quick lesson in longhorn virtues, in tones nearly as glib as the auctioneer's: "A seventh of the stock cows in the U. S. are first-calf heifers, and breeding them to longhorn bulls produces a long, thin calf that is easier to deliver. So you reduce a lot of veterinarian bills. And they're better eating. You see, the major beef cattle in this country—Herefords, Angus, and shorthorn—were developed in Britain when hides and tallow for candles were the principal by-products. Now people want cattle like these that produce lean red meat."

The horns, of course, command attention. A jittery cow, hyped by the crowd and the auctioneer's loudspeaker, spied a visitor near the fence and poked one between the wires at him as deftly as a boxer. The steers trotted into the show corral with 30-to-40-inch curved lances on their heads. They were bought as living artifacts of the Old West for about $1,200 apiece.

Receipts totaled a record $340,200, thanks to a young white cow that went for $32,000. "It was more than we wanted to pay," confessed Robert King of New Braunfels, Texas, who bought her in partnership with his neighbor Calvin Riedel. " But she had the ideal breed characteristics we want to develop in our own herds."

"Historical interest started the business in longhorns," I was told by Oklahoman L. V. Baker, president of the Texas Longhorn Breeders Association of America. "But then people began seeing their advantages as well, including high fertility. We feel that someday most herds in this country will have some longhorn blood in them."

When Karen Smith first started going to local dances in northwest North Dakota, she was approached by ranchers for the wrong social reasons. "I used to get a lot of static about the burning program," said the slender, handsome manager of Lostwood Refuge. Karen sets fires in rangeland, which ranchers see as taking grass from the mouths of cattle. She sees it as a way to restore native plants to Lostwood's 26,747 acres.

"Native plants are adapted to stress, from fire and occasional heavy grazing," she explained as we rocked over the undulating terrain in a refuge pickup. "When grass gets too rank, grazing prevents the formation of a thick mulch of dead grass which would gradually kill new growth. Burning eliminates any mulch and also reduces buckbrush, a low shrub that smothers and crowds out most everything else."

Her program calls for three sessions of burnings in multi-acre plots, every other year. Once the grass is reestablished, she says, burning may be necessary only once a decade. For thousands of years fires periodically seared the plains, some started by lightning and others by Indians. "They burned areas to create good grazing and attract the buffalo," said Karen. "We could let cattle do the grazing—some graze here now—but I can't find big herds to graze it closely enough."

Birds, not buffalo or cattle, are the major reason for restoring Lostwood grasslands now. Lostwood lies in a feature called the Missouri Coteau, a swath of rolling, dimpled land thirty miles wide and a thousand miles long, where slowly melting glaciers left soil and rock behind ten thousand years ago. Deep in every dimple is a small "pothole" of water, a springtime nursery for nesting waterfowl. Mallards, gadwalls, pintails, teal, and giant Canada geese nest in the grass, and their hatchlings feed on aquatic insects.

We topped a rise to see two army surplus jeeps driving across the prairie about 150 feet apart, dragging a cable between them. A research team from Fish and Wildlife's Northern Prairie Wildlife Research Center, at Jamestown, North Dakota, was looking for nests—one aspect of a study comparing the response of birds and plants to grazing and prescribed burning. I hopped aboard to watch.

A shoveler duck flushed, and we stopped to find her nest, a down-filled bowl so deep in the grass that the cable rode high over it. The team "candled" her 11 eggs, studying them against the sun to determine the embryo development, then flagged the spot to check again some days later. At a mallard's nest previously flagged, only shell fragments remained. "They were about one week from hatching last time we saw them," said biologist Jim Piehl. "Looks like the work of a skunk."

Skunks and raccoons will eat duck eggs; coyotes and foxes will kill and eat adult birds as well. Since men's activities have loaded the scales against a natural balance of predator and prey, man must control predators on occasion.

Many ducks will nest in the buckbrush, but its wirelike tangles harbor ground squirrels that relish duck eggs. There are other reasons for her brush war. "If you lose the grass," she said, "you lose wildlife associated with this northern prairie: Baird's sparrow, Sprague's pipit, upland plover—that's 'upland sandpiper,' the new name."

Since waving grasses have increased at Lostwood, some of the locals want to dance to her tune. "Now when I go to dances some people tell me they like what I'm doing here," she said with a smile. "A couple of ranchers have asked how they could do a burn on their pastureland."

A manager of a different era, Chesley Dinkins never worried about returning the prairie to its natural state. He's happy with the world he made at Lake Ilo Refuge, a three-hour drive south of Lostwood. On land once featureless and overgrazed, spruce, cedar, elm, ash, and ponderosa pine now rise like monuments near the 1,200-acre reservoir. Monuments, in fact, to the lifework of this grizzled 74-year-old with a round, impish face and an acid tongue. He was present at the creation, a foreman of the Works Progress Administration crew that built the dam across Spring Creek in the mid-1930s. When the resulting lake and the land around it became a refuge for ducks, deer, and pheasants, he became its manager—for 44 years.

"They tried to move me to others a number of times, but I wouldn't go," says Chesley, whose speech is as salty as it is blunt. He offers raspy opinions freely, on poachers or on "big shots" in government. The pioneers of the refuge system were his hunting companions—J. Clark Salyer, chief of the division of refuges from 1934 to 1961, and Ira Gabrielson, of the old Bureau of Biological Survey. Chesley's voice softens when he mentions his late wife, Polly, and the nine children who grew up on Lake Ilo's 4,033 acres.

"My wife came out here with me all the time," he said when I visited him, a few months before he retired in November 1983. "We hauled rock to build bridges and line the lake banks, built fences, and planted most of these trees by hand. The kids helped in summer. If I needed any extra help I'd just go into Dunn Center and get some of the boys. Now [voice rising] it takes a __-____ three months to hire someone by the time you have to fill out the __-____ forms and go through all the red tape."

Many of the trees planted by the Dinkins family are not native to the area. In this and other refuge practices he differs from those he snorts at as the new "college degree types." Burning rangeland, he says, seems like a "bunch of crap." And while most managers today believe that all creatures have a place on a balanced refuge, Chesley says, "I shoot all predators—skunks, coyotes, foxes—they eat the game animals." He detests coyotes in particular. "And I blast every goldanged son of a banshee that I see." Or words to that effect.

His wildlife philosophy aside, Chesley may be remembered for his versatility and thrift. He exemplified what another senior refuge manager called a "disappearing breed of supermen who could do it all." When the lake had to be drained to control rough fish years ago, he built his own siphon from barrels and saved the government hundreds of dollars. He once got approval to expand the manager's residence as his family grew, and requisitioned just $800. "Salyer told me, 'hell, I would have given you twice that much,'" Chesley related, "and I told him I didn't need any more 'cause I did the work myself."

If the production of waterfowl could be compared to that of automobiles, North Dakota would be Michigan. This northern prairie state is the biggest duck producer of the lower 48, and the focus of research on ways to produce even more with better nesting habitat. Some 20,000 ducklings a year are hatched on J. Clark Salyer Refuge alone, the Detroit of duckdom. With several new drainage projects that threaten to pour extra water onto the refuge, Salyer's staff now worries about being flooded out of the driver's seat.

Wetland drainage for agriculture affects an immense area. Thirty years ago the prairie pothole region, which extends from South Dakota and eastern Montana north to the boreal forests of Saskatchewan and Manitoba and Alberta, produced about thirty million ducks a year. It now produces fewer than twenty million. Darold Walls, Salyer's manager, took me aloft in a small plane to show me why.

We cruised over the refuge first, a green jewel of riverside timber and marshlands tied together by the meandering silver thread of the Souris River. Beyond refuge boundaries, the land in June is the monochromatic gray of tilled fields, spotted with the dark bruises of former water holes.

"Drainage is just killing this state," Darold shouted above the drone of the plane. "More than two million acres of wetlands have been drained from North Dakota alone. Besides providing habitat for waterfowl, potholes recharge the groundwater we use for drinking; they act as floodwater retention basins. But the people pushing for drainage see only the benefit to themselves—more farmland.

"This county already has about 300,000 acres in the federal Payment In Kind [PIK] program to cut back on wheat production. And now the county water-resource board wants to add nearly 7,500 acres of new farmland.

"In some cases public funds are used to drain lands to grow more grain—and then more public funds are used to deal with the surplus. Drainage aggravates flooding problems. The public is forced to build bigger or better dams to handle these floods. The real drain is on the U. S. Treasury."

Not only would the proposed projects dry up duck production and hunting areas, but they would also pour more water into the Souris, flooding nesting areas in the refuge. Someday, refuges may be the last resort for ducks seeking to raise a brood. So I was told, back on the ground, by Allan Aufforth, a barrel-chested, sandy-haired man with a bighorn sheep tattooed on one muscular forearm. A wildlife biology teacher at North Dakota State University at Bottineau, he is studying the vegetation around duck nests on grassy islands in the waters of Salyer Refuge.

"I'd hate to be a duck coming to this county looking for a place to lay my eggs," he said. "It's all black dirt with no cover. But tell that to a farmer who wants to drain a wetland to raise more wheat."

How particular is a duck about where she lays her eggs? I found out when we were joined by two soft-spoken specialists for a tour of Aufforth's study area. Harold Duebbert and George Swanson have been spreading the gospel of duck production for a decade, sharing knowledge gained at Northern Prairie Research Center with refuge staff. Duebbert takes a duck's-eye view of the perfect nest location. Swanson focuses on food for ducks and ducklings.

The conscientious duck, Duebbert explains, looks for nesting cover made up of tall grasses, weeds, or shrubs, thick enough to hide in and with an abundance of old growth that might discourage some predators. "To create attractive cover, I've found that a combination of cool-season grasses and legumes works best," he said as we waded into a meadow of waist-high herbage.

For an ideal nursery, add a protective barrier or moat. In a refuge airboat we blew to several islands to assess their value as nesting sites. "I remember an eight-acre island once that had 663 nests on it," Duebbert remarked.

Several ducks helicoptered up as we walked over the first island, which was covered with grass and prickly wild rose. A second, with similar cover, had not one nest. Duebbert looked around: "The dense cattails grow so close to this island that a skunk or raccoon could walk out here and barely get its feet wet."

Swanson gave us a short lesson in aquatic menus. "Look closely," he said, bending to the shallow water, "and you can see the small invertebrates—midges, side-swimmers, little snails—that feed the ducks. That sprinkling of green dots on the surface is duckweed, eaten by dabblers like gadwall. All these foods can be made available with good management."

But not, interjected Darold Walls, if silt-laden drainage waters pour in.

"We're pushing these buggers into smaller and smaller areas," added Aufforth, "and if we get a heavy fowl-cholera kill sometime with them all bunched up in refuges, the hunters can just hang the shotgun on the wall."

Mitch Kottas and Doug Krings of Lewistown, Montana, hung up the shotgun years ago and took up the bow. Hunting purists, they seek only trophy animals, and a record elk is the principal target. Bulls that other hunters would be proud to shoot have stood within a few yards of them, but when I joined them for a September hunt neither had loosed an arrow at an elk for two years.

"I guess you could call us fanatics," said Mitch, a square-jawed former track star. "We've both shot elk with guns, but there's little challenge in aiming through a six-power scope on a rifle that shoots accurately 300 to 400 yards. With a bow you have to get within 40 yards."

"It's not just killing an animal," added quiet, introspective Doug. "It's competing with one on its own terms."

Their main hunting grounds are the million acres of Charles M. Russell Wildlife Refuge in northeastern Montana, second largest refuge in the lower 48. In the system it's known as "CMR." Named after the self-taught cowboy artist of the Old West, it stretches along the Missouri River—125 miles by air, 155 by channel—through deep-gullied erosion known as the Missouri Breaks. The gullies, or coulees, with their sides and ridges sprinkled with ponderosa pines, and the river bottoms with their cottonwoods and willows, have hardly changed since the Blackfeet and the Crow and other tribes sought the plentiful game here. Mule deer, whitetails, and the stately elk remain abundant, as do badgers, coyotes, and bobcats, some 90 colonies of prairie dogs, and thousands of sharp-tailed grouse. In recent summers the most plentiful hoofed animals have been domestic cattle.

"We ran grazing surveys, and the cows were getting 60 percent of it," I was told by refuge manager Ralph Fries, a man quick to laugh but just as quick to defend the forage of his wild animals. "Our mandate says that wildlife should have priority. And if you talk about benefits to people, the numbers still bear that out. There're 92 ranchers who run cows on the refuge. But there are 300 gun hunters for elk and 2,500 for deer, and over a thousand bow hunters each year, and thousands more who come in summer just to see the wildlife."

In late 1983 a federal appeals court agreed, and the number of cattle on the refuge will decrease. The elk herd, however, will be kept at its present size, 1,400 to 1,800. When crowded, the big monarchs of the range wander off the refuge, break ranchers' fences, and compete with cattle for grazing on private lands.

Stephen Kellert of Yale told me that the general public seems to think of trophy seekers as headhunters who leave meat to rot. Kottas and Krings eat the animals they shoot, even though bull elk in the hormonal flood of full rut is not a gourmet's delight. "We don't affect the population much," said Doug, in defense of trophy hunting. "And the animals we want to shoot are well past their prime."

Like Captain Ahab pursuing the great white whale, they direct their zeal toward a large black-maned bull they call Garfield, for the county in which he was first sighted. The evening before the bow season opened, we lay on our bellies atop a ridge overlooking the Musselshell River, which feeds into the Missouri. With 16-power spotting scopes they scanned a maze of trees and grassy clearings.

"There he is," breathed Mitch. "Garfield. Take a look."

I put my eye to the scope and saw a kingly beast with a huge rack worn like a 30-pound crown. Between sessions of cropping grass, he herded before him half a dozen cow elk, to be defended in the coming rut.

We slept in a small camper trailer on the Musselshell bottoms. The alarm jangled at 5:30 a.m.; we donned camouflage suits and daubed our faces with green and brown paints. Unlike gun hunters, archers are not required to wear bright colors to avoid shooting one another by mistake. The one-shot chance and the need for careful aim make a snap shot at mere movement and shadows highly unlikely.

Doug took a stand in a dead cottonwood about a mile from camp, hoping Garfield would pass within range. Mitch and I prowled the edges of the clearings. This was hunting Indian style—stalking slowly, placing the feet carefully to prevent the snap of twigs, communicating in barely breathed whispers if at all. We sat motionless in heavy cover for half-hour periods before moving to another location. Once a young whitetail buck came within a dozen feet of me. The camouflage worked.

For three days, at dawn and dusk, we prowled the Musselshell bottoms. One morning, elk were so near that Mitch and I clearly heard the calves calling to the cows in mew-like squeals, but all were hidden by thick willows. Doug reported that a seven-point bull strode within 20 yards of his stand. But it was not Garfield, and Doug, who already has the tenth best bow-shot elk rack in the record books, let it pass.

The great black-maned elk, so easily seen with the spotting scope, became a phantom in the hunt. Another bowman reported later that he saw the bull enter a clearing with willow sprigs dangling from his antlers "like *he* was wearing camouflage!" Most likely Garfield had been sparring with a small tree to sharpen his fighting skills, but of such stuff are legends made.

Weeks later a letter from Mitch confirmed that he and Doug had another elkless year, although Mitch downed a whitetail buck that made the record books. Garfield, he reported, still lives. At least five arrows were shot at him, including one by Mitch that "hit heavy bone and got no penetration."

That was Mitch's explanation. With a phantom you can never be sure.

Indians were still hunting in the Missouri Breaks when the steamboat *Bertrand* cast off for Fort Benton in Montana Territory, in 1865. Two weeks out of St. Louis she hit a snag on the treacherous "Big Muddy" and swamped near the pioneering community of DeSoto on the Iowa-Nebraska border. Salvors may have removed most of the valuable cargo rumored to be on board, including gold coins and 5,000 gallons of whiskey. Silt quickly covered the *Bertrand*, and as decades passed the channel continually shifted. When the boat was unearthed in 1968-69, it was within the bounds of DeSoto National Wildlife Refuge, whose staff found themselves in the museum business. The *Bertrand* has become a time capsule of life on the frontier, with 150 tons of well-preserved cargo.

"It has been called the most complete collection of Civil War era artifacts in the world," said 30-year-old Suzanne Benda, a museum technician. "It has, to some extent, revised our understanding of what was available to people at those far western outposts."

Somebody out there was partying. The booty includes tableware: pressed glass, ironstone china, pewter, plated-silver cutlery. Among the foodstuffs are tins of oysters, and strawberries; jars of brandied cherries; powdered lemonade, and "essence of coffee," an early instant brew. And even without the rumored whiskey, the boat coughed up 941 bottles of champagne, 67 of whiskey cocktail mix, 2,921 of bitters—patent medicines of the day—and 189 bottles of assorted ales, wines, schnapps, and brandies to help ease the pain at civilization's edge.

A sampling of this astonishing variety is on display in a spacious visitor center, opened in 1981. Softly lighted, the neatly stacked curios appear as a mystic vision of a general store of the past, the racks of booze marching toward a blurry infinity.

DeSoto is much more than a historic gallery. As a wildlife refuge, it may have the most varied uses of all. Its main lake is a former oxbow, leveed off and supplied with sluice gates to control water levels. Fish and Wildlife agreed to allow fishing, motorboating, and waterskiing before it acquired any of the 7,823 acres. "The large urban population in Omaha and Council Bluffs has little available in the way of outdoor recreation," explained manager George Gage. Summer water activities have little effect on migratory waterfowl, he added.

With 3,000 acres of croplands, the refuge is a pioneer in the study of biological farming. Wildlife benefits from the 5 to 18 bushels of corn per acre left by harvesting machines, and also from the absence of insecticides. Farmers, tilling the land cooperatively, may benefit as well. Crop rotation in the bio-farming scheme has produced corn yields of 94 bushels per acre—a five-year average—in contrast to 90 bushels on adjoining plots using expensive petrochemicals.

Waterfowl and deer may be hunted in autumn. But the biggest hunt is in spring, when some 9,000 visitors tramp the woods in search of morels, the most delectable of the edible mushrooms, beige nodules with convoluted indentations that give them the look of tiny human brains. No one has successfully grown these fungi commercially, and morel hunters occupy an obscure niche of fanaticism. The location of their quarry seems to follow no sure pattern.

"Look around trees that have recently died," one morel hunter advised me.

"Trees that have been struck by lightning," offered another.

" . . . in a damp open field *near* the woods. . . ."

"Gnomes," said a refuge secretary with finality. "They come out at night and plant them."

This flurry of opinions was accompanied by a blizzard of puns. "Would you say the morel of the story remains a mystery?" asked one wag. Heh heh heh.

I headed into the woods with a veteran "moreller," Howard "Red" Marshall, a stocky, taciturn man in his forties with flaming curly locks and a thin mustache to match. He admitted to selling morels for $3 to $5 a pound to mushroom lovers who won't risk poison ivy and "itchweed"—stinging nettles. It's illegal to peddle mushrooms picked on refuge lands, but Red never said he sold any of those. Not even once did he say that.

The dead-tree theory worked, for a while. I headed for a leafless cottonwood with the boast, "Morels coming up . . . I can smell 'em." Not a one was coming up . . . and Red chuckled. "They ain't no guarantees."

I also found morels around live trees, in a grassy open field, and in a clump of young sumac—a baffling barrage of conflicting evidence. Could these brainlike fungi actually harbor a form of intelligence? If a foolish consistency is the hobgoblin of little minds, I seemed to be dealing here with genius.

DeSoto's 9,000 morel seekers pale by comparison to the 220,000 visitors drawn annually to the *Bertrand* exhibit. The five-million-dollar visitor center is the most expensive in the refuge system.

"Some people think that a facility like this saps money away from traditional activities of a wildlife refuge," said Dave Menke, recreation planner for DeSoto. "But we use the *Bertrand* story to help develop a historic perspective on land development. We show how items in the exhibit affected wildlife in the Missouri basin—how plows cut up the prairie, axes cut down the forests. The picks—mining, which silted the clear streams. The concentration of human populations in towns is represented by luxuries like china and champagne. Most of our visitors are from urban areas, and have a need for wildlife awareness."

Plows, axes, and picks from the past may help build that awareness.

So may a statement posted in the museum and attributed to an earlier American, an Indian chief named Seattle:

"What is man without the beasts? If all the beasts were gone, men would die from great loneliness of spirit, for whatever happens to the beasts also happens to man. All things are connected. Whatever befalls the earth also befalls the sons of earth."

In western wheatgrass on million-acre Charles M. Russell Refuge, Al Rosgaard—a wildlife biologist for Montana—holds a week-old mule deer. For a long-term study, state and federal colleagues will fit a radio transmitter to the fawn's neck and track the fawn and doe.

At a reservoir near Charles M. Russell, cattlemen round up their stock. In these dry grasslands, many ranchers need more acreage than they own, and have grazed their cattle on the game range since its founding in 1936. In early 1984, 84 graziers ran 22,000 cattle on CMR. But in 1983 a federal court upheld the priority of wildlife here, allotting only the excess forage to livestock, and the refuge began planning to cut cattle grazing by a third.

Piggyback means "chick-a-back" in the grebe family, and all six species of North American grebes breed in fresh water. Above, a red-necked grebe in breeding plumage ferries its young on a North Dakota pond—courtesy of J. Clark Salyer Refuge. To the northwest, at Des Lacs Refuge, birds of the dark and the light color phases of the western grebe swim side by side, and a pied-billed grebe paddles along with food for its young dangling in its beak.

PRECEDING PAGES: *American white pelicans nest on islands in Lake Bowdoin, where Bowdoin Refuge must manage a limited water supply to maintain its ponds and marshes.*

Tilled fields cup shallow ponds at Twin Lake Waterfowl Production Area (WPA) in North Dakota—a typical landscape of the prairie pothole region that stretches from South Dakota into Canada. Relics of the Ice Age, these wetlands support the highest concentration of nesting ducks in the lower 48 states. This region holds virtually all of the nation's WPA's, units which lie outside refuge boundaries and may have separate staffs but belong to the refuge system.

*Grassland vocalist, a grasshopper sparrow perches on
a dock plant and proclaims his territory: about two acres
of North Dakota's Lostwood Refuge. His song resembles
a grasshopper's buzzing. The little bird—weighing less
than an ounce—builds a small nest of dried grasses on the
ground where prairie plants conceal it. Green needlegrass
(below) frames a wild sunflower, a source of seeds that
many birds eat avidly. On Lostwood's original prairie,
controlled burning to reduce woody growth and encourage
native grasses will increase the habitat—and perhaps
the numbers—of the grasshopper sparrow.*

Past wooded breaks and rolling prairie, rafters float the Niobrara River in north-central Nebraska. Fort Niobrara NWR, where elk and bison roam, rims five river miles. From 1879 to 1910 its grasses fed cavalry horses; buffalo have bred here since 1913, descendants of a gift herd of six. The refuge sells about 70 calves a year to keep the herd at 225. In July the calves of both sexes, now several weeks old, sprout budding horns; and wood lilies blossom in the moist areas of woodland.

FOLLOWING PAGES: One of 50 elk on the refuge, a bull with antlers still in velvet lies in a field of coreopsis.

Lone reminder of his species' bloody past, a
bull at Wichita Mountains Wildlife Refuge
in southern Oklahoma evokes the days when
bison darkened the central plains. Six
hundred graze the refuge now—maybe more
than survived in the wild when President
Theodore Roosevelt proclaimed 61,160 acres
here a "game preserve." Other survivors of the
Old West endure today on 92 square miles of
mixed woodlands and prairies. Millions of
rangy Texas longhorns, descended from
Spanish stock, fed a growing country and
inspired cowboy legends. Then imported stock
on fenced-in pastures replaced the tougher
strain. "Since about 1922, the Texas
Longhorn has been nearer extinction than the
buffalo ever was," wrote Texan J. Frank
Dobie in 1940. To preserve the breed, the
federal government installed 30 of the animals
on Wichita Mountains in 1927; an annual
auction keeps the herd at 300. Below, through
wild rye and little bluestem, a wrangler
drives steers to corrals for inventory.

Sensing danger, black-tailed prairie dogs at Wichita Mountains tense at the entrance to their burrow. Once the foot-tall rodents, their underground colonies spreading for thousands of miles, probably outnumbered buffalo on the Great Plains. Farmers and ranchers have poisoned millions of the animals over the years, but they still thrive on protected lands. Wichita Refuge houses a town of 350 residents.

Yellowed grass and cholla cactus sweep to mesquite-dotted bluffs at Muleshoe Refuge on the high plains of northwest Texas. Established in 1935, Muleshoe originally sheltered wintering waterfowl. When rainfall decreased in the early 1960s, it began to attract lesser sandhill cranes, which sleep at night on the dry alkaline lakebeds. From October to March, thousands of them feed on insects and seeds in cropland that surrounds the refuge's 5,809 acres of shortgrass prairie. During the spring migration, watchers here have counted as many as 250,000 sandhills—45 percent of the mid-continent population. Only about 1,600 birds survive from an endangered race of the greater prairie-chicken. Rice growers have taken much of its habitat, but Attwater Prairie Chicken NWR in southeastern Texas preserves 8,000 acres of tallgrass coastal prairie. In early spring the males gather at communal display grounds called leks. To attract mates, a male inflates his orange neck sacs (below), then deflates them to produce a booming sound audible for a mile or so. About 200 birds survive on their special refuge. Such scattered parcels of sanctuary mark the croplands of the central states; in marked contrast, the refuge system owns and administers spacious—but menaced—reaches of the interior West.

THE

INTERIOR WEST

Snowcapped Mount Shasta dominates the skyline at Lower Klamath NWR on the border between Oregon and California. Established in 1908 by President Theodore Roosevelt as the United States' first refuge for migratory waterfowl, Lower Klamath and four others in the vicinity attract several million ducks and geese in spring and fall. About 500 bald eagles—the largest concentration in the lower 48 states—winter in this area. The refuges of the West loom as large as outlaw legend; those of the Klamath Basin alone contain more than 200 square miles.

FOLLOWING PAGES: A male sage grouse fans his tail and inflates air sacs on his neck during a courting display at Hart Mountain National Antelope Refuge in southeastern Oregon.

"There she is!" sang out Ray Paxton, nodding ahead and to the right of the pickup. "Hart Mountain." I was reminded of the "lost world" of Sir Arthur Conan Doyle—steep cliffs rising to a high flatland, suggesting an isolated realm of mysteries. This was southeastern Oregon, of course, not southeastern Venezuela, and Hart Mountain receives more than 20,000 visitors a year. The Scottish novelist's explorers found dinosaurs trapped in time, while tourists on Hart encounter creatures rescued from the past.

Pronghorn antelope, which are not really antelope but a species of ruminant unique to North America, were nearly wiped out along with the bison. Now they drop their kids on the sage-covered expanse of Hart Mountain Refuge. Sage grouse lurk in the wiry habitat that lent them half a name. The last native bighorn sheep on Hart disappeared about 1912, but a replacement herd from British Columbia thrives here.

In the interior West, the best wildlife refuges are monuments of rock and open sky. That slice of the nation which includes the Rockies, the intermontane area, and the Coast Ranges comprises roughly a third of the contiguous 48 states, but it looms larger in the imagination. The great vistas of the West shrink our egos and swell our awareness of the scope of the planet Earth.

We skirted the base of the 40-mile-long escarpment for a few miles before winding up a precipitous road with numerous switchbacks. At the top a broad plain stretched before us, sloping gradually to the Catlow Valley some 30 miles to the east, where more mountains fringed the horizon.

When Ray Paxton leaves his home in Lakeview, Oregon, and tops the last switchback to start another week as refuge maintenance man on Hart, he is, in a sense, returning home. "I grew up here," he told me, "back in the days when they had as many as 20,000 cattle and sheep running on this land. My dad worked for a ranch here, and I went to work at the age of ten. Grouse were so thick then that I could step off a hay rake and throw a hammer to knock one down for dinner.

"But the mountain was overgrazed. The grouse and antelope were disappearing, and there were bare spots where the land had been eaten right down to the bone."

In 1936 Hart became a refuge for a diversity of wildlife, especially pronghorn and sage grouse. Limited grazing continues—"politically it would be touchy to cut it out completely, and it does stimulate new growth," a Fish and Wildlife officer at headquarters in Lakeview told me. Meanwhile, the land and its wildlife have recovered.

Rod Blacker, assistant manager of Hart and a year-round resident of the mountain, accompanied me part of the way on an afternoon walk. "The overgrazing caused erosion and loss of good topsoil, so there's more sagebrush than we'd like to see," he said, long legs eating up the terrain. "But sage is important to pronghorn and grouse as food, and mule deer feed on it in winter.

"And here are bunchgrasses—needle-and-thread, and squirreltail," he added, bending to the ground. "This grass is *Poa secunda,* the same genus as Kentucky bluegrass. The yellow flowers are sagebrush buttercups and the yellow crownlike flower is wild parsley, like candy to grouse."

Rod turned back to attend to duties, and I continued to a rocky rise called Poker Jim Ridge. Distances are deceiving in the western vastness. My casual stroll became a six-mile hike, rewarded by the sighting of one mule deer, views from the ridge that stretched to infinity, and a long-distance look at some bighorns. My next walk would entail a closeup look at full-blown ardor.

At day's first light, in spring, male sage grouse gather on open grounds called "leks" to strut, swell their breasts, and battle other males. The eastern sky was faintly pink when Rod and I arrived at a camouflaged two-man tent he had set up as a blind two miles into the high desert. As we approached I heard a bizarre sound, somewhat like fluid being poured from a large jug.

When the light came up we saw dozens of grouse, the males strutting with all the pretension of a schoolboy swaggering across a playground. Occasionally one would draw air into two frontal sacs, causing the breast to expand till it nearly concealed the head. The wings drooped, the neck feathers ruffled, and the tail spread like a fan. In this puffed-chest posture the show-off would race forward a few steps while loudly rubbing his bristly breast feathers with the leading edge of his wings and forcing air from the sacs in the strange gurgling sound I had heard.

To the champions of all this bluff and bluster go the fair hens. "Sometimes a few subordinate males breed a few," whispered Rod, "but generally fertilization is done by the dominant males."

I trained my field glasses on a flurry of activity some 50 yards away, where a mature cock was chasing a younger grouse to remind him of his place. True combat involves pecking, and buffeting with the hard leading edge of the wing, and usually isn't needed once the dominant males have established their high status.

Above the racket of challenges and wing-drumming came the sharp bark of a coyote. Minutes later the animal trotted into view and eyed the activity but, strangely, came no closer. A red-tailed hawk soared almost to the midst of the lek, then winged away. Romance bore a charmed life this day, for both predators sometimes pounce on strutting birds, Rod said. Where grouse are concerned, love is truly blind. At least on Hart Mountain they have a chance to prove it.

Vast though the western lands may be, the collisions between man and wildlife are inevitable and continuing. At the National Elk Refuge in Wyoming, for example, animals have been crowded out of habitat. For centuries the protected spot east of the Tetons known as Jackson Hole has been a winter haven for thousands of elk. Homesteaders moved in late in the last century, and competition for natural forage grew keen. In the severe winter of 1909, thousands of elk starved. The refuge was established by Act of Congress in 1912, and the government has been nurturing the elk ever since.

Today the refuge totals 24,246 acres—about 5 miles by 10—and competition is from a new kind of homesteader, the homeowner of means and leisure. Refuge manager John Wilbrecht wants to increase the elk's winter range and migration routes.

"People say, 'Why do you feds want more land, you already own most of it in the area,' " he told me in his office one clear, cold February day. " But what we're losing includes the winter forage areas and the passageways into them. When you build right to the edge of the refuge you remove a certain amount of elk range. Elk are wary, they're going to maintain some distance from a house."

For good reason. Elk are hunted in Grand Teton National Park and the refuge in the fall, to keep the numbers manageable and hold down feeding costs. It cost $156,000, or $26.53 per animal, to feed the elk that wintered on the refuge in 1983. Part of that was borne by the animals themselves. Antlers shed by the bulls in March and April are collected by a local troop of Boy Scouts and sold at auction, and the receipts pay for supplies of elk feed.

At 7:30 the following morning we drove to a set of buildings a mile away and clambered onto a big six-wheel transport truck left over from the Vietnam War, loaded now with 20 tons of bullet-like pellets of compressed alfalfa hay. The food spilling from a trapdoor set the herd milling after us in a beige mass of antlered bulls, cows, and blunt-nosed calves. Some of the bulls sparred briefly, antler against antler, but these were chow-line squabbles, not the serious clashes of the rut. A few cows reared and, balancing perfectly on hind legs, windmilled front hooves at each other.

Each winter about 150 elk die on the refuge from old age, disease, hunting wounds, or accidental injuries. As the truck roared on, spilling its long line of pellets, a dark blotch lay unmoving on the clean snow near our starting point. A calf born the previous spring, now about 250 pounds, struggled to rise at our approach, but could not. "Probably trampled when they milled," said John. "From the looks of that one foot it was crippled and unsteady."

Two magpies flew down to the snow near the calf as we drove up. Would the refuge butcher the young animal, I asked, perhaps distribute the meat?

"No, we have coyotes, eagles, ravens, and magpies on the refuge," answered John, "and they have to eat too. When wolves were still around they pulled down the weak and sick. Now the coyotes just wait until they are dead."

Here the stark lessons of nature are not hidden from the numerous visitors. For a closeup look, they can climb aboard a horse-drawn sleigh, as I did, for a ride into the midst of a grazing, resting herd. The animals have learned that the quiet sleighs and clicking cameras pose no threat. Visitors, however, sometimes flinch at the sight of coyotes and eagles picking at an elk carcass.

"Sometimes people will say, 'Uh oh, I'll bet we weren't supposed to see that,'" said Mike Trumbower, young driver of the husky Belgian draft horses. "I tell them, 'Oh yes, that's exactly what you're supposed to see. That's part of the lesson: that nature is not charitable, but it is efficient.'"

Less acceptable are the occasional hunting cripples seen among the herd, often the victims of low-percentage chance shots.

While we fed a group of some 2,000 elk farther north on the refuge, a cow, obviously hurt, lay in the snow as if resting. Two coyotes waited patiently a few feet from her. Magpies perched in a cottonwood tree overhead. We dropped some pellets nearby, out of pity. She got herself up and hobbled toward them, and only then did we see that her left foreleg was shattered and useless. I wondered how many hunters would rush a shot at a game animal if they could see it months later, leg waving like a limp rag, starving in sub-zero cold.

The great majority of the herd, some 7,500 total, consists of splendid sturdy creatures, kept that way by the careful nurturing of grasslands during summer and the supplemental feeding for a few critical weeks in winter. An expensive, complicated undertaking, but a necessary compensation.

"Uh oh, I lost him." Wendy Brown yanked her field glasses to her eyes and gazed over the marshes and grasslands of Bosque del Apache. I had joined the energetic brunette researcher as she kept watch on five whooping cranes wintering on this refuge in central New Mexico—a phase of one of the most intensive bird watches on a single species in history.

It came into being when these tallest of North American birds fell to a total of 21 in 1941 (not counting two captives). Now the total population has reached about 140, a tentative reprieve from oblivion helped by placing whooper eggs under greater sandhill cranes, which raise the hatchlings as their own. Dutifully following their foster parents, several white-plumed youngsters now stalked the wetlands of the "woods of the Apache."

Isolated in the Chihuahuan Desert, sheltered by the Chupadera Mountains, watered by the Rio Grande, Bosque's lush vegetation harbors a wide variety of highly visible wildlife. In this popular "drive-through" refuge I saw plentiful song- and shorebirds, bald eagles, four red-tailed hawks hunkered over a duck carcass, and, at evening, double-digit numbers of mule deer. Plus a blizzard of snow geese.

Gadwall, pintail, and northern shoveler ducks and Canada geese are seen in abundance on Bosque's man-made lagoons but the snow geese, sometimes totaling 30,000, are the main show. Once I saw them, alarmed by a military helicopter, rise in a mesmerizing white cloud, rattling the air with plaintive cries. Flying singly or in small groups, black primaries rowing alabaster bodies through the air, they resemble . . . whooping cranes.

The possibility of that confusion explains why Wendy Brown fretted over a wader that had slipped away. Early February was snow-goose hunting season on the refuge in 1983. Dropping her field glasses, she snatched up a field radio and said, "Headquarters, I've lost one of the whoopers. It might be heading your way. Keep an eye out for it, will you?"

In 1983 Nita Fuller was acting manager, running the Bosque hunt. Goose hunters there must attend a two-hour school and pass a recognition test of snow geese and whooping cranes. They are parceled out, three hunters to each of twenty blinds, with a radio receiver for every blind so hunters can be warned if a whooper is in the area. Nevertheless, one whooper was found wounded in January 1984—shot off Bosque land—and the status of hunting at Bosque is uncertain now.

"I have no problem with hunting geese on the refuge," Nita Fuller told me. "We get more every year, and hunters take only about a thousand. As for the whoopers, we feel that we're sensitizing a lot of people to watch for them."

In the darkness before dawn I joined businessmen Phil Brenfleck and Roe Souther in the number 13 blind, a small fort of straw bales in a refuge wheat field. We set out 112 decoys, then settled in for a four-hour wait in biting cold. As light came up the snow geese began flying high over us en route to grainfields, and the radio crackled at 7:03 a.m.: "You may begin hunting."

Carrump! Carrump! A few guns fired in the distance. Phil made honking, chuckling noises into a wooden goose call, but no birds came into range. "Our best hope is to bring in a few juveniles that don't know any better," he said, with a few break-off squeaks like the cracked tones of a teenager's lament. No takers.

Hours passed. Feet grew numb. Sandhill cranes rowed overhead, trilling their soft *ker-loos*. The radio warned blinds 4, 5, and 6 that a whooper might be in their area. Phil honked a heartbreaking soliloquy of goose loneliness, and was snubbed. At 11 a.m. the radio announced the end of the hunt.

"It doesn't bother me, not shooting a goose today," said Phil as we picked up the decoys. "It's a privilege just seeing them fly over. We'll probably go to the refuge this evening and watch them come in to roost, whiffling and talking to each other."

"I enjoy the refuge hunt," said Roe. "The school and the tight control tend to eliminate slob hunters—those who blast at anything at any distance and if they knock it down say, 'Hey, I wonder what this is?' "

She loves reptiles beyond reason and prefers campfires to casinos. No child of the city, my daughter Lisa. Only a day earlier she had dabbled in the world of slot machines in Las Vegas. Now she dabbled with a stick in the coals of our evening campfire and watched the mountains of Desert National Wildlife Range dissolve into blue-gray. "Just two hours apart," she said contentedly, "two entirely different worlds."

Some 12,000,000 tourists pass each year through the glitter capital of the nation. Only 12,000 visit the largest wildlife refuge in the lower 48 states, 1,500,000 acres devoted principally to the preservation of the desert bighorn sheep. It begins just beyond Vegas city limits and stretches roughly 60 miles into the Mojave Desert, through broad, cactus-studded valleys and up barren, shimmering mountains. Two hours from the rattle of dice to the skittering of a spiny lizard through the dry leaves of a creosote bush . . . or the hollow moan of jet fighters playing at war. Part of the refuge also serves as a bombing range for the Air Force. Ah, the desert, land of contrasts.

"The planes make their runs in the valleys and the sheep are generally on the ridges," I had been told at refuge headquarters in Las Vegas by assistant manager Earl Kisler. "There's very little ordnance dropped any more."

"I had field glasses on a group of sheep once when planes caused two sonic booms a few seconds apart," said his colleague Bruce Zeller. "The first one they ignored. The second was the kind that jars your teeth, and some of them raised their heads. Maybe it's like thunder to them."

"We don't know the effect on the sheep," added manager Bob Yoder. "We can only speculate that it is not positive."

The herd of 1,700 on Desert Refuge is one of the world's largest collections of desert bighorns. Fewer than 100 tags are issued for hunting them each year. Hunters are schooled in selecting only rams over seven years old—"on the downside of life"— by horn curl and horn growth rings. Slightly more than half the hunters manage to bag one. Smallest of America's bighorn sheep, the desert race is also the wiliest, as Lisa and I would discover in our attempts to observe them. Our closest look was from the air.

We went aloft in a Huey helicopter with Zeller, Bill Burger, a graduate student at Humboldt State University in California, and an Air Force crew of three. Burger is studying seasonal movements and habitat use by following radio-collared sheep. The Air Force, in the spirit of restitution for their low-level bombing runs and their noisy dogfights, periodically provides a helicopter for the project.

Guided by the beeping in Burger's earphones, we hovered a few hundred feet off awesome mountain faces. A young ram raced headlong across a bulge that ended in a thousand-foot drop, a sight that left a void in my innards. A group of eight ran to a pinnacle and paused, looking back to where we hung in the air. Precipitous terrain is the mountain sheep's protection. Our bellowing whirlybird seemed to render it useless, and the animals' confusion was plain.

We located four of five collared sheep, but saw only two. Sheep are known to remain still, their drab color blending into rock, or hide in caves. Extraordinary eyesight gives them early warning. "I've made 75 or 80 sightings of them from the ground," said Burger after we had landed, "and in all but five cases when I located them with field glasses they were already watching me."

As they must have watched us later. For three days Lisa and I hiked the heights near our camp in Joe May Canyon, looking for sheep on their own terms. Although they eluded us time and again, the visit to their high realm had its rewards. Unspoiled peaks marched away to the horizon. Distant Las Vegas looked like ant rubble on the desert floor.

Weights, more than heights, bother me on mountains. Tons of boulders and cracked cliff faces above me, waiting for their millennium to join the valley below, fill me with unease. As we struggled upward at 7,000 feet below such an avalanche-in-waiting, three jarring sonic booms from unseen fighter-bombers rent the air—a hammerblow of unwelcome vibration.

In this first truly warm spell in April the valley floors came alive with lizards, delighting the 21-year-old reptile lover with me. It was in a valley, in fact, that we finally spied our quarry.

Walking up a dry wash late one morning, we spied several light-colored lumps half a mile ahead. Field glasses revealed a dozen sheep moving away from us and a ram standing sideways, studying our every move. We sat on the ground, backs against a rock, and watched them work their way up a slope. The climbing seemed effortless, but at any pause one or more would plop down for a rest. When they finally disappeared over a high saddle we gasped our way hurriedly to the top, but they had vanished in the forest of seemingly endless rock. For one of America's most furtive mammals, there are plenty of places to hide.

Later, as Lisa dropped to her stomach to commune with a horned toad, I studied my maps to see how much ground we had covered. We had walked miles each day, scaled mountains and crossed valleys, but if the map were the size of my spread hand, we had penetrated the refuge far less than the length of a fingernail.

A different kind of wild life invades Havasu Refuge on the Arizona-California border. Topock Gorge, an 18-mile stretch of the Lower Colorado River with pea-green clear water and spectacular scenery, becomes a summer habitat for water-sport fun-seekers. "Some of them drive 300 miles in their $25,000 cars, pulling their $15,000 boats," said one refuge official. "They get on the river and get beered up and, frankly, sometimes they're not very nice."

Law enforcement patrols keep refuge personnel in the field long hours from Memorial Day until Labor Day at Havasu. Armadas of jet boats scream between the rock bluffs. Jet skis—like aquatic snowmobiles—ply small coves the wide-hulled boats can't enter. Raucous noise to an endangered bird so secretive that refuge workers have to trick it into singing to make a population count.

Yuma clapper rails may number only 1,700 in the world, with about 250 of them at Havasu, acting manager Dick Gilbert told me as we putted along the Colorado in a refuge motorboat. "They live in the marshes," he said. "They're nonswimmers, but they thread their way through the cattails, eating mostly crayfish."

At times a landing would have been impossible as the current flowed past multicolored stone that rose on either side for hundreds of feet. Beneath the overhang of one wall, cliff swallows clustered like moths around mud-daubed nests. A swimming pair of western grebes, sophisticates with ruby eyes and slicked-back heads, dived haughtily at our approach.

Where silt had taken hold, the green of cattails and bulrushes fringed the shores. We burbled into a quiet inlet and cut the motor. Gilbert pushed a button on a tape recorder and played territorial cries and love songs of the Yuma clapper rail. An answering call is logged as a bird count. "They rarely show themselves," he said, "but this method works for a census."

A stiff breeze this day had created a symphony of its own in the grating of marsh stems and the swish of leaves. "I doubt that they can hear the recording," he finally conceded when no answers came.

The call of the gorge has long drawn man to its cathedral beauty. Gilbert tied up at a willow and led me to a rock face scratched with Indian petroglyphs. Mule deer and bighorn sheep, along with plentiful waterfowl and squawfish, probably supplied the red men here. But in the gorge, the scream of jet boats is a far cry from the scratch of petroglyphs. "We can't imagine that the noise is good for the rails and the mountain sheep," said Gilbert. "But these are navigable waters, and under present laws we can't stop the boats."

After another dispute over refuge priorities, the Secretary of the Interior ordered the Bureau of Reclamation to stop dredging activities on the river. Both FWS and the governor of Arizona had argued that the spoil piled along the banks ruined wildlife habitats. Glitches between governmental units are not uncommon. Farther north in California, what began as a model of cooperation has produced a nightmare.

Genetic nature had run amok. Creatures from a science-fiction horror show appeared before me in a darkened room at the University of California at Davis. A grebe chick with beak twisted and hanging down as if it had melted. A duckling that looked normal except for a webbed foot which was upside-down. A black-necked stilt with no wings, no legs, no eyes, and a beak turned back on itself.

"Survival is poor even with less obvious abnormalities," said Harry Ohlendorf, a Fish and Wildlife biologist who studies the effects of contaminants on wildlife. "They limit the young bird's movement and ability to feed."

He shut off the projector and switched on the lights. Relief surged over me, as if I were emerging from a bad dream. For FWS officials at Kesterson Refuge, two hours southeast of San Francisco, the dream won't go away so easily. Ponds on the refuge have become contaminated with an element called selenium, almost certainly responsible for the deformities we had just seen.

The pollution of Kesterson is no familiar story of industrial carelessness, of callous dumping of waste products or the leaky disposal of toxic effluents. Selenium, a chemical element found naturally in soil, is beneficial in minute quantities. In humans, at levels of 52 to 100 micrograms a day, it counteracts deficiency symptoms, such as some heart problems. In large amounts it counteracts normality. Ironically, its invasion of the refuge is a result of measures to enhance one of the most fertile and productive areas in the West.

The San Joaquin Valley in central California turns out more than 99 percent of the domestically produced raisins eaten in the U. S., a fourth of those eaten in the world. Navel oranges and 98.7 percent of this country's marketed nectarines are harvested there, as well as large crops of almonds, walnuts, wheat, alfalfa, and cotton. Irrigation is the key to this productivity, and the villain for Kesterson.

Irrigation water must be flushed out after it has been applied in the valley, to prevent salt accumulation in the soil. In 1968 the Bureau of Reclamation began building the San Luis drain, a concrete-lined canal to carry used water to the San Francisco delta. Congress issued new directives and construction stopped in 1975, so the water wound up in a series of ponds. A sensible plan was developed: The valley would be drained and FWS could raise some ducks in the resulting wetlands of what is now Kesterson Refuge. It didn't work that way.

"Selenium is highly soluble in alkaline or salty water, so the salty irrigation water leached it from the soil," explained Ohlendorf. "When the water was dumped in Kesterson, the selenium was absorbed by plants and insects and thus entered the food chain. Coots seem most affected of our species—42 percent of their nests have abnormal young."

As we talked, a phone jangled on Ohlendorf's desk. He answered it, then covered the receiver and said: "This is our chemistry lab in Maryland. They've been analyzing for selenium content in the breast muscle of ducks on and off the evaporation ponds. Everybody wants to know if we should advise hunters against eating them."

Returning to his call, he took down figures between a string of "uh-huhs" and hung up. Was that a tiny smile I saw, the researcher's fascination with truth, no matter how gruesome?

He turned the sheet around and pointed to his tallies: "These three samples came from an area with normal levels of selenium in the water, and they averaged a half part per million. These others came from the evaporation ponds and had from two to nine parts per million."

Nine parts per million, in a one-pound portion of affected duck from Kesterson, equals about 4,000 micrograms of selenium.

Early in 1984, California health officials issued an advisory: Young children and pregnant women should not eat any coot from the refuge evaporation ponds; others should eat no more than one per week. Arthur Kilness, M. D., who has studied selenium for years, says simply: "I wouldn't eat any of those ducks."

Kesterson includes 1,000 acres of wetlands and 3,400 of grasslands that the runoff does not enter. But for now, the ponds at the end of the San Luis drain continue to collect selenium—as studies continue on its effects. A noble venture to promote wildlife has turned into a giant laboratory to study toxic aberrations.

What a piece of work is man! He flushes fields, levels forests, carves waterways, creates swamps, drains swamps, changes the courses of rivers. But at times his surgery on the land seems the work of a brilliant surgeon operating with a hatchet and buck knife, his mistakes and excesses sutured with leftover string.

At the turn of the century the Klamath Basin on the California-Oregon border was a fertile zone of shallow lakes and vast marshes, swarming with waterfowl. In fall migrations, great flocks out of the north were funneled there by Oregon's high country and the towering peaks of the Cascades. The numbers of concentrated ducks and geese were estimated in the millions.

Less than two decades later most of the basin had been drained and dried, the rivers that fed it diverted. Lower Klamath Lake, observed refuge pioneer Ira Gabrielson, "was a pitiful remnant of its former magnificence, and its companion, Tule Lake, was rapidly approaching that condition."

In 1908, Lower Klamath Lake became the first waterfowl refuge. Tule Lake joined the growing system in 1928, and today the Klamath Basin complex includes four other units as well. Still, less than 25 percent of the old wetlands remains.

Nobody told the ducks and geese. For decades they continued to swarm into the basin, devouring the farmers' grain. Bill Sellers, who came to the basin as a high school student in 1942, remembers clouds of birds over Tule Lake. "They took about 25 percent of the grain," he told me in a trailer serving as a check-in station for waterfowl hunters. "Farmers would pay a kid a dollar an hour and provide the ammunition for you to 'herd ducks' off their crops."

Waterfowl still descend on crops in the basin, in far diminished numbers. Tule Lake Refuge, for example, totals 39,396 acres, but by Act of Congress almost half of that must be leased to farmers on a cash-payment basis.

"Essentially, our complex is set up for bird migration, so we set restrictions with that in mind," said Klamath manager Bob Fields at the complex's gleaming new headquarters at Tule Lake. "Farmers cannot plant more than 25 percent of their leased land in row crops; and no more than 10 percent of the stubble ground—wheat, oats, and barley—can be fall-burned or plowed, so the birds can forage on dropped grain."

In the gray half-light of a rainy October dawn, assistant manager Homer McCollum and I cruised the sticky bottomland of Tule Lake in a refuge pickup, on a patrol of goose-hunting activities. For the first two days of the hunt, "when the birds are still dumb" as Homer put it, the number of hunters is restricted—600 at Lower Klamath, 800 at Tule Lake. After that it's wide open.

Homer McCollum's face remains impassive, his mouth barely moving when he talks. The most telling expression on this transplanted Missourian exists in his eyes, where a secret mischief often dances and pirouettes. "Hunters are not a bad lot," he said as we rolled past a leftover potato field where white-fronted geese pecked at remnants of spuds. "People who don't hunt think of them as callous. But I've seen guys who look so rough you'd swear nothing ever passes their lips but meat, and they'll come back to the check-in station with tears in their eyes, talking about geese flying against the rising sun."

No geese darkened one corner of a wheat field where four hunters stood upright next to their decoys. As our pickup rolled to a stop near them, one of the men said disconsolately, in what must have been a paraphrase of a refuge brochure, "Thousands and thousands of geese are not coming to us."
Homer's eyes did a quick jig: "Well, fellas, to a goose you probably look an awful lot like a bunch of hunters standing around their decoys waiting to shoot something. You might do better to push up a little mound of straw and get behind it, or get down in that plowed ground where you won't show up so well."

"You know," he said as we drove on, "most of the people who hunt here only get out five or six times a year, so you can't expect them to be very good at it. They want the fresh air and recreation, to get away from the city awhile. But it's getting harder and harder to get a bird, because bird numbers are way down from 10 or 15 years ago. And small bunches are much warier than big ones."

A skein of white-fronts coasted overhead, their family babble drifting down to us. All over the marsh, small groups of ducks and geese formed dark hieroglyphs against the gray sky. A field away a 12-gauge thumped twice at a landing straggler, and a light mist of birds rose from the ground. A mist, not the cloud of waterfowl that Bill Sellers had remembered from his high school days. How much had the flocks diminished, I asked Homer.

"You're looking at a third of what was here in the early '70s," he answered. "And a fifth or sixth of what was here in the '50s."

Why?

"It's easy to blame the other guy—the Eskimos up north are shooting them in spring, or the Mexicans down south in winter. Now there's a tendency to fault the data, to say the original estimates were exaggerated.

"But it always gets back to loss of habitat. In California alone there's been a drop in wetlands from 5,000,000 acres to about 300,000. You don't winter a lot of birds in housing developments and cotton fields." I turned quickly and looked for the pirouette in his eyes, and it was not there.

Was there any chance, I asked, that the same government that now pays some farmers not to grow crops might buy back land to restore wetlands? And the waterfowl along with them?

Homer stared out over the steering wheel. "That land was bought at, say, 15 cents an acre years ago by developers who drained it and sold it for $15. Now if the government wanted to buy it back it might go for $5,000 an acre, and in the meantime there are people who make a living off of it.

"No, we'll never get those birds back again."

Four-foot rack of antlers crowns a tule elk wading at California's San Luis Refuge. Once thousands of these smallest of North American elk roamed the San Joaquin Valley. Fewer than two thousand remain—53 of them here, in one of the last remnants of their traditional habitat.

Mat of dried algae blankets a dried-out pond on Kesterson Refuge in the San Joaquin Valley. Water drained from farmlands to the south contains salt and other minerals, among them the element selenium. Occurring at toxic levels in ponds that cover 1,300 acres on the refuge, selenium causes waterbirds' chicks to develop with missing or malformed eyes, bills, wings, and legs. Below, in a lake at the refuge's edge, a scientist collects mosquito fish (bottom) for chemical analysis. Some invertebrates survive here, but no other species of fish can live in these waters.

FOLLOWING PAGES: A mixed flock of lesser snow geese and their smaller cousins Ross' geese fills a misty December sky above Sacramento Refuge in California. Three million waterfowl —about a third of those that migrate along the Pacific flyway —winter in the Sacramento Valley.

Bunchgrasses offer good grazing on the hillsides of the National Bison Range in western Montana, where a bull wanders alone. Bighorn sheep prefer flower heads of the arrowleaf balsamroot (below), which blooms in spring—at lambing time. The refuge shelters bighorns, elk, and pronghorns as well as the buffalo, now 300 to 400 strong. In 1908 the American Bison Society paid $10,560 for 12 bulls and 22 cows to stock 18,500 acres which the government bought from the Flathead Indians for $30,000.

Male and female trumpeter swans, mates for life, watch over their cygnets at Red Rock Lakes NWR in southwestern Montana. Ranging into Idaho and Wyoming, the "tri-state" trumpeter population stands at about 450 birds. Federal biologists knew of fewer than 100 at the founding of this 62-square-mile refuge for them in 1935. Opposite, at nearby Lima Reservoir, a trumpeter watches a Fish and Wildlife Service employee band its leg. Bands identify the resident flock. Others visit in winter: 800 to 1,000 of them, some from Canada. At left, in the refuge's drier grassland, a Richardson ground squirrel suns itself on a rock ruddy with lichen.

Snow-dusted mountains of the Wasatch Range form a backdrop for a flock of American avocets at Bear River Migratory Bird Refuge in northern Utah. On impoundments such as this one, the 64,895-acre refuge regulates water flow to maintain levels ideal for shallow feeding. Below, a black-necked stilt pauses in its search for aquatic insects. As many as 5,000 of this species alone gather here each August.

DENNIS R. DIMICK, N.G.S. STAFF (BELOW, BOTH); LARRY R. DITTO (OPPOSITE)

Cuddly-looking porcupine contemplates its next meal of willow shoots at Malheur Refuge in southeastern Oregon. A wide variety of birds and mammals lives in its 282 square miles of marshes, ponds, lakes, and high desert. Above, an August moon rises over Hart Mountain at the National Antelope Refuge. Two pronghorn fawns follow their mother as other does and a buck cast wary eyes over the sagebrush range.

Rising on powerful wings, greater sandhill cranes fly above Bosque del Apache Refuge in New Mexico. Below, taller, whiter, and far rarer whooping cranes mingle with sandhills on a refuge cornfield. Since 1975, selected pairs of sandhills have served as foster parents, hatching whooper eggs from northern Canada or from a captive flock at the Patuxent Research Center. FWS personnel carry the eggs to sandhill nesting sites in heated suitcases. If successful, the experiment will shorten the whoopers' migration route, increasing the chances of survival for this endangered species.

Stately saguaro cactuses reach toward redrock outcrops at Kofa Refuge in Arizona. Below, refuge employee Ron Kearns measures plants of this Sonoran Desert habitat: thick-leaved desert agave; spiny-armed buckhorn cholla; spindly wolfberry; yellow-flowered brittlebush—a rich diversity in a land where high ground may receive as much as eight inches of rain a year and other areas get less than three.

ALASKA:

A LAND APART

Throngs of common murres swarm over a patch of food-rich water in Kuskokwim Bay off the coast of Togiak NWR in southwest Alaska. The feeding frenzy, a sure sign of large schools of fish, attracts a gill-netter out for herring. At sea, the common murre hunts underwater, diving as deep as 30 feet. Ashore, huge colonies of murres crowd the sea cliffs, where females lay single eggs on the bare rock. In summer, seabirds by the million migrate to coastal rookeries on Togiak, one of the 16 refuges in the state.

FOLLOWING PAGES: *Bellowing fiercely, Steller's sea lions react to a boat approaching their rookery off Nunivak Island in the Yukon Delta Refuge. Sociable as well as curious, these mammals haul themselves up on land in spring to mate, give birth, and raise their young.*

STEVEN C. KAUFMAN (LEFT AND FOLLOWING PAGES)

We've been given another chance. The refuges elsewhere in the U. S. were mostly salvaged from land badly eroded, heavily logged, drained dry, or seriously overgrazed. We brought back wildlife where it had been obliterated, or defended the few that somehow had survived. In Alaska the refuges were started before despoliation gained a foothold. Habitats are being preserved, not restored; populations of creatures that use them are being protected, not rebuilt.

The Native peoples—Eskimos, Aleuts, and Indians—are given consideration. Under the Alaska Native Claims Settlement Act of 1971 they may own and live on land within refuge boundaries, hunting and fishing for subsistence. A precedent from the nation's infancy might have been an Act of Congress designating whole Eastern states as game-management units and letting the Mohawk, Delaware, and Cherokee continue their way of life.

Theodore Roosevelt established six Alaskan bird "reservations" in 1909, and by 1971 some 22 million acres were in refuges. With passage of the Alaska National Interest Lands Conservation Act (ANILCA) in 1980 the total more than tripled.

" The refuges here are 180 degrees from those in the lower 48," I was told by Judy Liedberg, formerly a recreation planner for FWS, now with the National Parks. "Down there they're closed to public use unless the manager says otherwise. Here they're open unless the manager says otherwise. Alaskans insisted it be that way."

Then why call them refuges at all?

"If the wildlife or habitat in them ever does become threatened we'll have some control," answered Dave Stearns, manager of Tetlin Refuge, southeast of Fairbanks. "Our mandate is pretty clear. We were handed a piece of the ecosystem and asked to maintain it without losing any species or altering the habitat."

Saving habitat sometimes means letting nature destroy it . . . temporarily. With Stearns I was flown into Tetlin to document the effects of a forest fire allowed to burn more than five weeks the previous summer. For half an hour the intense green of Alaskan spring flowed beneath us, laced with rivers, dotted with pools. Four times we spotted moose feeding on aquatic plants. Then the landscape ran black and barren until our amphibious plane splashed down in the sky-blue waters of Takomahto Lake.

A summer-long fire raises eyebrows in Alaska, among hunters and trappers. "We have to convince them all that in the long run a burn will benefit them, with increased browse and more game," said Stearns as we set up camp in a mossy glade spared by the fire. "But we've got to have data to back up our claims."

With assistant manager Steve Breeser we walked a mile of the burn area, studying the recovery of land and creatures at several marked stations, or transects. An equal number are inventoried in an unburned area for comparison. "I've been surprised at the birds that are already in the burn," said Breeser. "Dark-eyed juncos, yellow-rumped warblers, olive-sided flycatchers, ruby-crowned kinglets, robins, gray jays."

Our walk stirred up fine ash that blackened our legs to the knee. At every transect Stearns threw down a hoop two and a half feet in diameter—roughly one ten-thousandth of an acre—and we knelt to see tiny green shoots of revegetation. "Two percent grass, 10 percent mare's tail, a showing of birch, 25 percent litter, and the rest is ash," observed Stearns.

Three mousetraps baited with peanut butter were set at each transect, and some had snapped shut on small red-backed voles. "We want to know how quickly rodents appear," explained Stearns. "One theory is that they're attracted to herbaceous plants and grasses in a burn area, which would mean an early influx of predators such as pine martens, lynx, and fox—all valuable fur animals. If it's true, trappers shouldn't mind having a burn once in their lifetime."

On a helicopter flight out we stopped at an Indian trapper's abandoned camp, littered with a cast-off dogsled and a splintered and sun-bleached pair of snowshoes. Mute testimony, Stearns pointed out, to the march of technology as the snowmobile replaced older forms of transportation. Later I would hear from Native Alaskans how their lives have changed.

The plane roared and shuddered and finally broke free of the water clutching at its floats. Bethel shrank beneath us, every packing crate, snowmobile, and cannibalized car body exposed to view. Then Hangar Lake and the treeless town and civilization's flotsam were behind us, and a mosaic of green and blue stretched in all directions.

I had joined assistant manager Mike Rearden and wildlife biologist Vernon Byrd on an aerial survey of tundra swans and white-fronted geese. The white-fronts I had seen at Klamath Basin in the fall probably hatched in Yukon Delta NWR, along with emperor geese, about half the continental population of the western brant, and all the small Canada geese known as cacklers. Ducks include scaup, red-breasted mergansers, the common and the spectacled eiders, oldsquaws, green-winged teal, American wigeon, pintails, and black scoters. Passerines sing in the willows, and shorebirds cry in the shallows. Each summer Yukon Delta becomes a concert hall, but the music is growing fainter.

America's biggest refuge has nearly 20 million acres, a roadless, boggy expanse built by the state's two largest rivers. The Yukon meets the sea at the north end, the Kuskokwim at the south. In winter, when darkness yields a few begrudged hours to dimness, the land between is a howling, snowbound plain; in summer, a nursery to millions of birds. Year-round it is home to about 18,000 Eskimos who hunt nesting waterfowl—and eggs—in spring.

Beyond the refuge's 19.6 million acres, an additional 7 million have been designated as Native selections. Completing a formal survey of the area, resolving such questions as conflicting choices, and perfecting the paperwork of transfer will take years if not decades. Eventually the Eskimos may own something like 25 percent of the delta area, with the right to range and hunt over the rest. "One of the reasons the refuge was formed was to sustain a Native subsistence life-style," explained Mike Rearden, pilot of the floatplane. But since 1964 the area's Native population has doubled, and motorboats and shotguns exact a greater toll than kayak-borne hunters armed with spears and nets.

In the mid-sixties a decrease in waterfowl was noted. In the late 1970s an internal FWS memo warned that the future looked bleak for several species of geese. Hunters and public officials are discussing remedial measures. Nature's part in this is beyond control—spring storm tides flood the nests and kill the unhatched chicks.

Both time and tide seem to be overtaking the Natives. From a society based on kinship they have surged to membership in corporations that purchase hotels, real estate, and fisheries. Strangers to a cash economy, they need cash to buy the snowmobiles and motorboats, the guns and ammunition that make life easier.

Flood tides years ago harried the Eskimos of Chevak until they moved to higher ground along the Ninglikfak River, about ten miles from the coast. It was foggy and raining intermittently when Mike Rearden left me on a muddy bank at the edge of town. The small shapeless houses, the endless, flat landscape, and the lack of trees gave Chevak a tentative look to me, but its residents feel a distinct sense of permanence. They also know the poignancy of change.

"The old ways are gone forever, so we've got to get the best deal we can for us and our kids," said Leo Moses as we sat around a table in his house, munching on dried salmon dipped in seal oil. His English is almost as fluent as his first language, a dialect called Cupik. "If that means letting the oil people drill, then oil it must be."

Derricks and pump stations on his beloved tundra?

Leo lowered his eyes and mumbled, "I'm 50 years old and don't have much time left anyway." His 24-year-old daughter Linda, a student at the University of Alaska at Fairbanks, spoke up: "Maybe it would mean we would have running water, and more job opportunities. Of course, maybe there will be three times as many people wanting those jobs." In the delta the future sometimes seems as foggy as a summer day.

As we strolled Chevak's boardwalks, the taste of seal oil still on my tongue, I asked Leo what they ate besides fish in the long winter. "Salmonberries and blackberries last quite a while," he said. "And my wife and I dig up 'mouse food' in fall—the grass roots that mice store for winter. It makes a good stew when boiled with seal fat and fish guts." Just then we met a young girl carrying three ice-cream cones in one hand and a six-pack of Pepsi-Colas in the other.

"We need to arouse the young people's mind about what was good about those old ways," said Joe Friday, the town elder or "honored one." He sat on an aging overstuffed couch in his little living room, a tiny, wizened man carrying the wisdom of many delta winters. "People have individualized themselves. Love and sharing, helping each other used to be important," he said. "Now if a healthy man sees an old woman chopping wood he thinks, 'well, that's her business, not mine.'"

"Would you like white wine or beer with dinner?" asked Leslie Kerr. I thought she was joking. "White wine," I told her, "but only if it's chilled." It was. In mud. Four of us were camped on a sandbar of the Nowitna River during a tour of Nowitna Refuge, newly created by ANILCA. Traveling by canoe allowed us the luxury of insulated coolers for beverages and perishables. Chunks of permafrost, sealed in plastic bags, kept them cold.

The 1980 law calls for each Alaskan refuge to be studied and a "conservation plan" to be drawn up by 1987. Leslie, a landscape architect by training, was taking her first closeup look at one of the four refuges for which she must devise such a plan. Charlie Blair, acting manager of Nowitna and at that point its complete staff, came to familiarize himself further with his responsibility: a land nearly 400 square miles larger than Delaware. Archaeologist Charles Diters came along to assess any potential archaeological sites.

Nowitna's forested lowlands are sprinkled with marshy lakes, rich in fish and waterfowl. Moose feed in the pools in summer. Marten, lynx, beaver, and black bear are plentiful, and there are foxes and wolves as well. In this state the refuges can still protect entire healthy ecosystems.

There are no roads. The four of us were flown upstream, canoes lashed to the plane floats. Then for three days we paddled with the current through raw wilderness unblemished by human use. A cow moose and her small calf plunged into the water for a crossing only yards from us. A big bull eyed our approach and melted into the trees. "Most of the moose hunting in Alaska is done from rivers, so the meat doesn't have to be carried far over land," said Charlie.

Near the river's junction with a brook, a swirl caught his eye. "That was a nice one—let's get some dinner." We swung the canoes to shore, and within ten minutes had landed three sheefish—a kind of whitefish, each weighing eight pounds or more. Several times we stopped, although often Charlie gently released his catch. "I want to

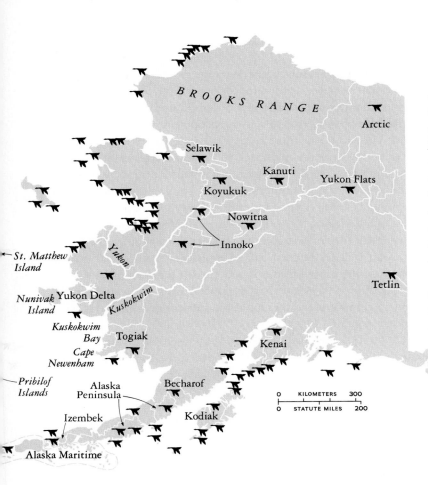

Arctic

Selawik

Kanuti

Koyukuk

Yukon Flats

Nowitna

Innoko

St. Matthew
Island

Yukon

Tetlin

Nunivak
Island

Yukon Delta

Kuskokwim

Kuskokwim
Bay

Togiak

Kenai

Cape
Newenham

Pribilof
Islands

Alaska
Peninsula

Becharof

Izembek

Kodiak

KILOMETERS	
0	300
STATUTE MILES	
0	200

Alaska Maritime

Scattered across the great virgin wilderness of Alaska, 77 million acres of refuge area promise protection to a spectacular array of birdlife and mammals. The Aleutian Islands, an 1,100-mile arc in the Pacific, form the heart of Alaska Maritime NWR, which holds some bits of coast as well as many coastal islets. The Alaska Lands Act of 1980 created nine new refuges and consolidated others in a measure that nearly tripled the size of the entire system.

see what fish are available, and in what abundance," he said. We ate samples of his inventory every evening.

At the confluence of the Nowitna and the Titna we beached to claw our way through dense willows and underbrush, calling "hey bear!" to avoid surprising that often irascible creature at close range. Our goal was a riverside cabin for Charles Diters to assess. "Built in the 1920s according to the wire nails, probably by a gold miner," he concluded when we found it. "It has no historical value, unless one finds 'Jack London slept here' carved in a log wall."

The Nowitna is one of 25 Alaskan rivers designated as wild and scenic. Leslie views the stream as a "corridor of use" and must describe in her plan activities that would not detract from its primitive beauty. Nowitna Refuge is a virgin resource, free from the strains of middle age and heavy use.

But you can drive to Kenai Refuge. The fact is mildly shocking, given the remoteness of most refuges in Alaska. Three hours by car out of Anchorage will bring you to Soldotna, a fast-growing town of 3,353 with a new 27-store shopping mall, obviously for visitors. Signs direct you to refuge headquarters and a visitor center. I felt I was back in the Outside.

"We're more like a refuge in the lower 48 than any other in Alaska," said manager Bob Delaney, "because of our accessibility. That makes us a testing ground for the kinds of problems all Alaskan refuges will face some day."

Half a million people flock to the Kenai Peninsula each year. Several hundred thousand visit the refuge to fish, hunt moose in autumn, hike some 100 miles of foot trails, float on rafts down the Kenai River, paddle the canoe trails, or park in authorized campgrounds. In summer the driving circuit on refuge grounds resembles a "galvanized ghetto of recreational vehicles," according to one refuge officer. Moreover, trapping permits are issued on demand, and several dozen oil wells dot the grounds, urged to more production by a hissing, roaring gas-injection plant.

Under this human impact Kenai must keep a close watch on its wildlife populations, which include some 5,000 moose and about 80 wolves. Alaskans eat moose as if they were wild cattle. Biologist Ted Bailey explains one consequence: "Wolves are regarded as pests that kill these cattle. It's unfortunate that one of the species we have the least of, here on the refuge, some people want most fervently to reduce."

The Moose Research Center on Kenai is studying calf mortality and nutrition needs. The refuge totals nearly two million acres and appears lush with greenery, but the size is deceiving, as Bob Delaney pointed out. "People don't realize that it takes five times the area up here to support wildlife as it does further south, because we just don't get as much vegetative growth in our short summers. Even our waters are less productive; we don't get enough warm weather for heavy nutrient growth, so it takes a trout much longer to reach large size."

Which may account for salmon mania. When the red salmon are running upriver to spawn in early July, anglers stand elbow to elbow in the Russian River and boat traffic on the larger Kenai River suggests the evacuation of Dunkirk. A lifelong angler who has paid his dues in sardine-size catches, I eagerly shared a boat and guide with three other people to try the giants of Alaskan waters—the king salmon. For hours we powered from one spot to another, to drift with the current as our treble hooks baited with globs of fish eggs tumbled along somewhere below.

The salmon disdained my line, cleaving instead to that of a 100-pound student lawyer from Anchorage named Nancy Nolan, who had never hooked a fish before in her life. Hers was a monster half her weight that bent her pole double and tripled the size of her eyes. For nearly half an hour she hung on gamely, cranking in the unseen weight while the rest of us ingloriously clung to her coattails so she wouldn't be pulled overboard. Finally a gleaming silver 52-pound torpedo lay flopping in the boat.

A Jonah swallowed by despair, I settled for helping devour Nancy's first fish back in Anchorage. I, and about two dozen of her friends.

Beneath a perfect sky, surrounded by unspoiled wilderness, we walked in a flawless hush. Four tiny mortals making our way, ant-like, through a vast amphitheater that seemed to have no beginning and no end. A chartered Cessna 185 had landed us on a gravel bar in Arctic Wildlife Refuge, and then quickly roared away. The valley lay ahead and behind, a mile-wide trench between mountains velvety with moss. The crests marched on 35 miles north of us, ending in tundra that sloped another 20 miles to the Beaufort Sea. To the south lay more mountains, and more, and more, bearded with spruce and birch and willows farther south and threaded with rivers that drained into the mighty Yukon nearly 200 miles away.

We worked our way up the valley of the Kongakut River in one of the most isolated areas remaining in the United States, the Brooks Range. Barbara had joined me for the trek, her first long backpacking experience. Nancy Nolan, the Kenai angler, was tasting this time the formidable emptiness of the unsettled far north. We were led by Macgill Adams, a blond-haired, blond-bearded professional guide.

For ten days we would define a leisurely loop of about sixty miles, changing camp every other day, exploring in between. A few Dall-sheep hunters fly in, we were told; Eskimos and Indians hunt the fringes of a tract larger than Switzerland, Belgium, and half a dozen Liechtensteins. If ever I felt transported to a new, unpeopled planet it was here, where the vastness says Alaska and the purity rinses the soul.

Beauty above ground, oil below. ANILCA authorized seismic exploration for oil and gas within Arctic Refuge, but required Congressional approval for drilling. Fish and Wildlife officers monitor the seismic work to avoid the "thermokarsting" of the 1950s—scarring of the tundra with tracked vehicles so the permafrost melts and slumps into a wide ditch. Ecologists view with concern the prospect of helicopters buzzing over caribou calving grounds. The work will take place on the North Slope, on only 1.6 million of Arctic's 19.026 million acres. But more disturbance may follow. "With oil activity," says Ave Thayer, former manager of Arctic Refuge, "more and more pilots learn the weather patterns and begin to explore, finding landing sites. More and more hunters come. That soon changes the nature of a wilderness."

Change has yet to come. Only three times in ten days would we see evidence of other humans: the contrail of a jet; the distant wreckage of a small plane; one set of boot prints in the mud. Mere moments, in days of natural wonders.

We had missed the migration of the Porcupine caribou herd—totaling some 140,000 animals—to the North Slope calving grounds, but we did see scattered groups of bachelor males, grazing on the slopes or resting on river ice, seeking respite from swarms of mosquitoes.

For days the only sounds were those of birds, our own voices, or the breakup of ice on the Kongakut—a roar like crashing boxcars. Some 175 miles above the Arctic Circle, the sun never set on the tundra, and it rained on us just once. We awoke to a succession of dazzling clear days that never darkened, only grew less bright around midnight. The air was scented with lupine, bell heather, and labrador tea.

In this world of crowds, true isolation can be nearly incomprehensible. The mind barely accepts what the map shows as vacant for a hundred miles in any direction. Several times I shushed our group and swore I heard tractor engines, some vestigial hum of civilization, only to draw laughter from the others.

On a day-hike, Barbara and I started up the tussocky flank of a peak that towered over the rest. Before long we were clambering over piano-size fragments of this earth-wrinkle that had collapsed on itself. Was still collapsing, I worried, nursing my dread of avalanches. Through the *irk* and *gronk* of protesting stone we panted upward, finally reaching the top with the elation that comes from conquering not the mountain, but the fear of it.

A cavalcade of peaks and valleys and streams marched to all points of the compass, a staggering sweep of grandiloquent emptiness. A world visited infrequently by man. The remotest valleys doubtless sheltered creatures that would live out their lives without sighting a human being. I never heard the tractors again.

During the 12-mile traverse of a lesser valley we stumbled across the skulls of six Dall rams. From the curl of the horns, none had been less than eight years old. All would have been worthy trophies—but all had died, apparently, of old age. Three days later, on another mountain, Barbara, Nancy, and I saw two dozen of the living white skywalkers, scampering nonchalantly along suicidal paths.

The last leg of our loop took us into an American Shangri-la with green hills on one side and chocolate-colored slate mountains on the other. Despite uplifted spirits, not everything was heavenly. Full-pack marches were often marked by aching shoulders, by silent prayers that a breeze would blow the bugs away.

All the complaints you might have heard about Alaskan mosquitoes are inadequate. Head nets and rain suits kept them off, but were hot. Repellents discouraged them, but not for long. They crashed into our coffee, kamikazied into our evening stew when their feeding frenzy was matched by our own. My only satisfaction came when I examined one with a small magnifying glass as it gorged on my blood and spied tiny orange mites clinging to its legs. Ah, so they also had tormentors.

We cooked and ate 75 yards from our tents, and piled food bags downwind before we slept. This was grizzly country; we didn't want to bait them near us. The first one flushed from brush a quarter mile ahead and hot-footed it over a mountain. The next two, lolling indolently in the sun, let us walk within 50 yards.

"There's a bear," hissed Macgill, stopping suddenly. "No, it's two bears. Oh my God." Meeting a grizzly at close range can be trouble. Meeting two compounds the problem as protectiveness or jealousy enters the picture.

They had not seen us. We were backing off to work our way around them when a dislodged rock went *klunk*. One of the grizzlies reared upright, front paws dangling daintily against its chest, and looked at us. Then it *woofed* and both fled across the creek and crashed into the willows.

I have met bears in parks that regard humans with brazen and dangerous insouciance. The grizzlies' mad flight was a reminder, a heart-thumping one to be sure, that they were unused to human presence, a reminder of the nature of the wild. Few refuges can lay claim to the exclusivity of Arctic, although by Congressional mandate the welfare of wild animals within all of them should carry the highest priority.

The well-being of the national refuge system, inevitably, will depend upon the knowledge and concern of America's citizens. It has become more significant to me. For months it has been my privilege to walk the paths of the refuges, ply their waterways, and enjoy the company of as dedicated a collection of federal workers—or any workers—as I have ever encountered. "There's something almost pure and ennobling about working with wildlife and trying to preserve it, that shows in the quality of those involved," a latecomer to FWS once summed up for me.

Once nearly ignored, refuges are now being pressured for economic development, for use as recreation, and by the general crush of human habitation. Even the people running them are changing. With more scientific training, they are also increasingly urban by upbringing; older hands of rural origin fear this may make them more tolerant of human intrusion.

"Refuges used to be inviolate," said biologist-photographer and retired manager Luther Goldman. "I don't want to deny anyone the experience of them, but it bothers me to see so many people pass through them now."

Does public use build awareness of wildlife, or detract from wildness? That's arguable. Few can deny, however, that the refuge system is mankind's most emphatic nod to the value of this planet's nonhuman inhabitants. That we continue to hunt them may be immaterial; survival has always been their business. Nature requires a fair chance for them, however, with places to hide and reproduce so they can continue their quiet acceptance of the cycles of want and plenty, of joy and fear, of life and eventual death.

Perhaps it is to learn that acceptance from them, to keep our own detail-crowded lives in perspective, that we seek their preservation.

At home in the high ridges of the Kenai Refuge, a pair of ewes and a young Dall sheep rely on surefooted agility and keen eyesight to elude predators—including man. Trophy hunters prize the rams for their curling horns. All national refuges in Alaska allow hunting; state game laws set bag limits and regulate the hunting seasons.

STEVEN C. KAUFMAN

Casting for red salmon, anglers line up in the Russian River in the Kenai. Only 110 miles by road from Anchorage, the refuge draws half a million visitors annually. Here sportsman Arnie Taggart from California poses beside a bull moose he brought down. Many Alaskans count on moose as a source of meat. Hunters may take 400 Kenai bulls a year, usually the biggest and best; natural predators would choose smaller, weaker specimens.

BOTH BY STEVEN C. KAUFMAN

Mountains unnamed and barely explored dominate the interior of Kodiak Island, where roughly two-thirds of the land belongs to the namesake refuge. Despite this bleak terrain, sedges, grasses, and berries provide forage for the massive Kodiak bear, as heavy as 1,700 pounds. In summer the refuge population of some 1,800 bears grows fat on salmon that swim upstream to spawn. Below, in a fight over a fishing hole, two Kodiak bears joust in its icy water. Concentrations of salmon bring these generally solitary animals into contact, triggering combats for dominance. Young bears—less than four years old—may spar merely in play.

In bachelor bands or alone, musk-ox bulls rove Nunivak Island until the rut. Confronting danger, these animals stand side by side, ready to use their horns. This tactic, sound against wolves, proved suicidal against men with firearms, who killed them off in Alaska before 1900. Herds today descend from animals imported from Greenland in the 1930s. Some 500 musk-oxen flourish on Nunivak, part of the Yukon Delta Refuge. Recently the state allowed limited hunting when their numbers threatened to exceed the limited grazing capacity of the land. At left, alert to intruders, a pair of oldsquaws rest on the island turf. The long pointed tail and the pink-banded bill identify the male of this common northern sea duck.

Meandering across a water-logged landscape of its own making, the mighty Yukon River winds through Yukon Delta Refuge to the Bering Sea. The immense plain constitutes one of the major waterfowl breeding areas in North America. Framed by tall sedges, a white-headed emperor goose and her three goslings will migrate to the Aleutians in the fall. Most of the world's emperor geese nest in the refuge, also noted for its salmon streams. At her summer fishing camp, Eskimo Purdy Olrun watches her son place a plastic tarp over chum salmon and trout drying on a rack. In rural Alaska, Native cultural tradition and sheer human survival may depend on subsistence hunting, trapping, and fishing; Congress has authorized such activities on most federal lands.

ALL BY STEVEN C. KAUFMAN

Early summer in the Brooks Range: In the mountainous heart of the Arctic NWR, Eagle Creek twists darkly through bottomlands still buried under the river's overflow ice in June. A lone cow (below), from a herd of some 140,000 caribou, rests on the snow-frosted tundra. Each year the caribou migrate hundreds of miles across the range, traveling to calving grounds on the North Slope, then south again for winter. Other mammals also roam far and wide to survive on the slim resources of the tundra. Only through its vast size—second only to Yukon Delta in the entire system—can this refuge of more than 19 million acres ensure adequate habitat for its wildlife.

ENTHEOS (ABOVE); LOWELL GEORGIA (RIGHT)

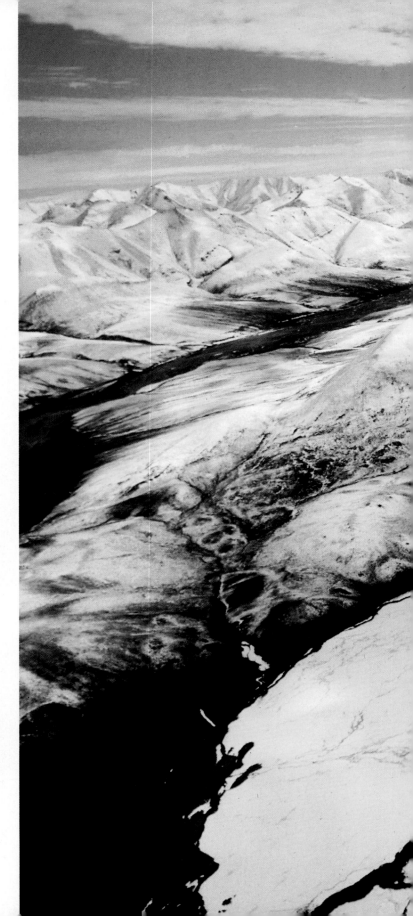

On a rocky shore in the remote Pribilof Islands, a northern fur seal nourishes her pup. About a million seals converge each spring on these ancestral breeding grounds. Native holdings apart, Alaska Maritime NWR has jurisdiction here. The refuge includes uninhabited St. Matthew Island, where an arctic fox howls defiance. At the end of the fleeting summer, its coat will turn snowy white. Meanwhile, high clouds reflected in a freshwater pond hint of a storm to come after a rare clear day.

Winter visitors from Asia, whooper swans rest on a shelf of ice in the Aleutians, within the Alaska Maritime Refuge. The large yellow patch on the bill distinguishes these swans, normally found nowhere else in North America. Notorious for fogs and gales, the islands have a relatively mild climate; they offer as many as 350 whoopers a haven from Siberia's sub-zero cold. Some 15 to 20 million seabirds find shelter on or around the rocky isles and islets of the chain—eastern edge of a migration route for Asian species, and a nesting ground for birds of the Pacific rim. This refuge and others protect the astonishing natural world of Alaska; they affect the complex web of life that unites all wild creatures and the planet earth.

Acknowledgments

The Special Publications Division gratefully acknowledges the generous assistance that men and women of the U. S. Fish and Wildlife Service have given us during the preparation of this book. In Washington and in regional offices, at refuge headquarters and in the field, their cooperation has been invaluable. Many specialists, at the Smithsonian Institution and other centers of learning, have helped with points of detail. In addition to the individuals, groups, and agencies named, portrayed, or quoted in this book, we thank those cited here: Nell P. Baldacchino, Michael Boylan, Elizabeth Dudley, Richard J. Hensel, Wayne Hill, Gerry King, Tom Smylie, George E. Watson.

A Researcher's Note and Additional Reading

"An unfertilized flower on a melon vine waiting for a passing bumble bee. . . ." So "Ding" Darling characterized the refuge system in its early years. Then it was hardly a system—it was a potpourri of sheltered parcels, lands set aside for wildlife with no coherent program of management. It evolved in a haphazard, pragmatic manner. Even its designations varied greatly, such as "bird reservation" or "game preserve." President Roosevelt in 1940 brought an end to this muddle, stating that it was "fitting and desirable that the names of such Federal areas should distinguish them." He officially changed most of them to the standard "national wildlife refuge."

More muddle surrounds the number established over the years. Many were created, then abolished. Some were transferred to another federal agency or to a state's jurisdiction; still others were absorbed by larger refuges. More than a hundred have become non-refuges. Two-acre Palma Sola in Florida, set aside in 1908, was dissolved in 1948 after the island had eroded away. Alaska Railroad Muskrat and Beaver Refuge, established in 1927, was released in the '50s for homesteading by veterans of World War II.

For those that endure, official sources sometimes conflict. Date of establishment may be reckoned from authorization—by Act of Congress or Executive Order—or from the first purchase of land. Acreage figures may or may not include water surfaces within refuge boundaries; they may vary because of surveying techniques. Some refuges, such as islands or remote expanses, have not yet been surveyed. Alaska figures are further complicated by Native selections, a process that may take decades.

The complex of refuge lands continues to grow. As of July 1984, it embraces 421 national wildlife refuges, waterfowl production areas amounting to 1,700,000 acres, and 58 coordination areas (tracts used by state authorities for wildlife purposes). It now totals some 90,000,000 acres.

Surprisingly, no definitive history of the system exists. Much material lies uncollated in refuge files. The central files of the Fish and Wildlife Service contain a wealth of particulars, not yet fully indexed. Two overview books are informative, but dated: *Wild Sanctuaries*, by Robert W. Murphy (1968), and *The Sign of the Flying Goose*, by George Laycock (1965). More recent is the handbook *Guide to the National Wildlife Refuges, How to Get There, What to See and Do*, by Laura and William Riley (1979).

"Blue Goose Flyer," a quarterly newsletter published by the National Wildlife Refuge Association, P.O. Box 124, Winona, MN 55987, discusses current refuge issues and includes useful information on the lands and the people who manage them. Articles on refuge lands often appear in the publications of such groups as the National Wildlife Federation, the National Audubon Society, and Defenders of Wildlife.

The *National Geographic Index* lists articles on these sanctuaries and the species they shelter. *Our Threatened Inheritance*, the Society's new large-format Special Publication, discusses some of the threats to the refuge system today; its companion volume, *Guide to Our Federal Lands*, contains helpful information on what to do and see at many refuges.

In addition, Fish and Wildlife publishes a directory of refuges and many other free publications on the sytem. Direct your inquiries to the Office of Public Affairs, FWS, Washington, D. C. 20240. If you are planning a major vacation trip or serious wildlife-watching, you may wish to contact local refuge headquarters well in advance. Certain areas may be closed, for instance, at nesting season. Local staffs can recommend the best times to visit and the best methods for viewing.

Conservationist Aldo Leopold, a motivating force and inspiration for the emergence of these lands as one system, said that "Conservation is a state of harmony between men and land." Whether through natural or artificial devices, refuges strive to realize this harmony. They serve wildlife first—but also bird-watchers, students, hunters, or simply seekers of solitude.

Guarding his territory in nesting season, a red-winged blackbird perches on a convenient signpost at J. Clark Salyer NWR. For many species, the blue goose symbol means "protected habitat." For U. S. citizens in particular and for all lovers of wildlife, the refuge system stands guardian of a living heritage that humankind can defend— but could never re-create.

BARBARA A. PAYNE

INDEX

Library of Congress CIP Data
Grove, Noel.
   Wild lands for wildlife.
   Bibliography: p.
   Includes index.
   1. Wildlife refuges—United
States. 2. National parks and reserves—
United States. I. Littlehales, Bates. II.
National Geographic Society (U. S.).
Special Publications Division. III. Title.
QH76.G76   1984   333.95'16'0973
84-16539
ISBN 0-87044-477-8
ISBN 0-87044-482-4 (lib. bdg.)

Composition for Wild Lands for Wildlife by National Geographic's Photographic Services, Carl M. Shrader, Director, Lawrence F. Ludwig, Assistant Director. Printed and
bound by Holladay-Tyler Printing Corp., Rockville, Md. Color separations by the
Lanman Progressive Co., Washington, D. C.; Lincoln Graphics, Inc., Cherry Hill,
N.J.; NEC, Inc., Nashville, Tenn.